# Adobe InDesign 2024

## For Beginners

The Comprehensive Guide to Unlocking Adobe
InDesign's Power to Create Professional
Layouts and Designs

McBunny Albert

# TABLE OF CONTENTS

# INTRODUCTION

Hey there, design enthusiasts and creative minds! Get ready to embark on a visual adventure with our Introduction to Adobe InDesign 2024 guide. We're going to explore the fascinating world of design, and InDesign will help you turn your thoughts into stunning works of art! Imagine a tool that makes it easy to design beautiful brochures, interesting documents, and attention-grabbing digital publications. That's exactly what Adobe InDesign is for, and this guide will make it all easy for you. There's no fancy language here, just plain old creative fun! We can help you whether you're an expert in design or a beginner. This guide is like having a best friend in design. It shows you all the coolest features, secret tips, and hands-on lessons that will quickly turn you into a design pro. This guide is like a pen, and InDesign is like a blank paper. We'll look at the newest and best features, figure out how to make smooth designs, and make your creative ideas come to life. It's not just about buttons and tools; it's about giving you the power to make magic that looks amazing. Hold on tight for a trip where design meets ease and each click gets you one step closer to letting your imagination flow. Hello, and welcome to Adobe InDesign 2024! This is the place where your design dreams come true and your ideas fly.

# CHAPTER 1
# ABOUT ADOBE INDESIGN 2024

Adobe InDesign 2024 is the newest version of the software. It has a lot of cool new features and changes that make it even better than the last version. This makes it even more of the industry's favorite desktop publishing tool. InDesign 2024 is a big deal for both artists and marketers because it has a lot of new tools and makes it easier to use. Let's look at some of the great things about this release that make it a must-have for creative workers. A Look at Adobe InDesign 2024: Adobe InDesign 2024 is the tool you should use to organize and design materials for books, magazines, catalogs, templates, and pretty much anything else you can think of. When it comes to planning plans for multi-page documents, it shines. It's great for single-page projects like flyers and posters. With the ability to work with text, pictures, and drawings, InDesign 2024 is the best tool for making documents that look good and are uniform. Designers can count on this app's professional and useful tools. It has font features that are similar to those in Illustrator, Photoshop, and other Adobe Creative Cloud apps.

InDesign has changed over time. It used to only work with print documents like business cards and ads, but now it can do a lot more. Thanks to Adobe Digital publishing plugins, it can now be used on multiple platforms to make dynamic documents like PDFs and publications that can be read on screens like the iPad and Android. For those who are already familiar with the basic text options in Microsoft or Adobe software, importing Microsoft Word or Excel documents is a snap. Formatting text is also simple. Advanced Typography and Design Options: InDesign has a lot of tools that can help you improve your design skills. You can easily make general changes to your project and set text styles to automatically edit text. You can easily add visual effects like drop shadows or glows to multiple pictures and change how they look. InDesign can't open some different picture types and works well with Adobe apps like Photoshop and Illustrator that use the same file formats. You can also improve your design by adding things like a QR code or an automatic table of contents. Easy Export and Approval: When you're done with your work, InDesign lets you send it to clients as a low-resolution PDF that can be sent by email. You can also pick from high-resolution PDF options that meet the standards of the current market. A powerful and easy-to-use design tool, Adobe InDesign 2024 is not only simple to learn but also fun to use. No matter how experienced you are as a creator or how new you are to the field, this release has something for you.

## Overview of key feature updates

### Auto Style

Adobe Sensei is a more advanced form of AI and machine learning technology that is used by InDesign's Auto Style tool. Users can simplify and streamline text formatting with this feature, which lets them make and use style packs. These style packs, which are groups of paragraph styles, make it easy to use the same layout across different text frames in a document. Users can make their custom style packs or pick one of the 20 style packs that Adobe has already made. This adaptability meets the design needs and tastes of people working on a wide range of projects. The Style Packs area in InDesign is where users can go to get to the Style Packs features. This area is where all of the management and application of style packs to text frames happen. From the menu, users can choose "Window," then "Styles," and finally "Style Packs" to find the Style Packs panel. Users can quickly choose which text frames they want to style once they are in the Style Packs panel. The next step is to pick a style pack that was already made or one that you made yourself. This easy step-by-step process makes text editing faster and easier, giving the whole paper a more professional look.

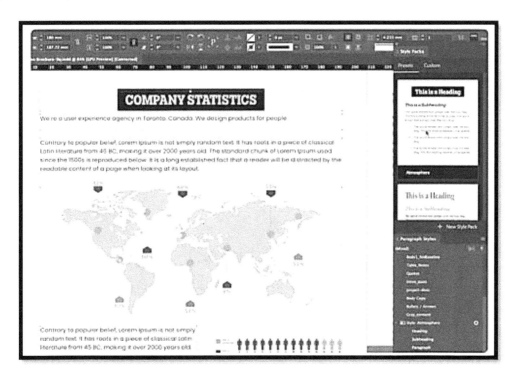

## Hide Spreads

Once you're done styling the text frame in InDesign, you might find it useful to hide some spreads in your document. Thank goodness, InDesign now lets you hide spreads. This gives you more control over what content people see during slideshows or when you share documents.

**These easy steps will hide a spread:**

1. **Get to the Pages Panel:** In InDesign, go to the Pages panel. Tap the "**Window**" menu and then you can choose "Pages" to get to this screen.
2. **Choose the Spread You Want to Hide:** Find and choose the spread you want to hide in the Pages window. You can hide a certain spread by clicking on it.

3. **Right-Click and Select "Hide":** Once you've chosen the spread, right-click it to bring up an option. Pick the "Hide" option from this list. This move will hide the chosen spread for good.

Now that some spreads are hidden, when you share or show your document, only the pages that can be seen will be included or shown. This feature gives you more freedom by letting you change the content that is shown during talks or when you share documents with other people. This feature comes in handy when you want to focus on certain parts of your document or when you want to share a document with information that is meant for different people. By hiding spreads, you can make sure that the presentation is more focused and organized, which will help your design or information get across more clearly and effectively.

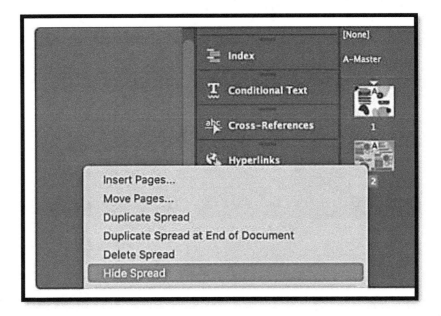

## Filename Suffix

Adobe adds Filename Suffixes, which give users a strong way to organize their files and make file handling easier. With this feature, you can add certain endings to your file names, such as page numbers, step numbers, or page sizes. By adding these endings, you can quickly find and sort your saved pictures based on what they are meant to be used for, which will speed up your work. **If you want to use the Filename Suffixes tool in InDesign, here are the steps:**

### Step 1: Accessing the Filename Suffix Feature

- In InDesign, go to the "File" menu.
- Go to "Export" and select "Format." Then, pick JPEG or PNG as your chosen picture file under the "Format" option.

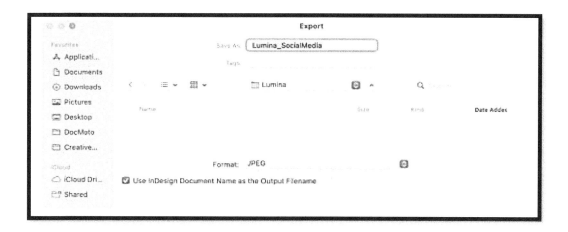

## Step 2: Adding Suffixes to the Filename

- Find the "Suffix" field in the "Export" part.
- Click on the "+" sign to start adding an ending to the title.
- Based on your organization's needs, pick the ending options you want, such as step numbers, page numbers, or page sizes.
- After configuring the ending options, click "Export" to produce the saved pictures with the designed filenames.

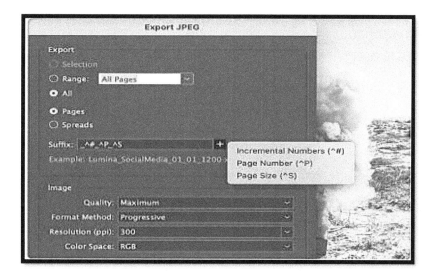

It's especially helpful to have this tool when making pictures for social media and other sites. One example is when you are creating pictures for different social media sites that have different size standards; you can use suffixes to make the sizes different for each site. This makes sure that the pictures you send are well-organized and can be quickly identified by the purpose for which they were created.

# Publish Online

The Publish Online tool in Adobe InDesign 2024 makes it easy for artists to share their products and designs on the internet. With this tool, designers can use InDesign Publish Online to make digital versions of their work, which comes with a full set of tracking data. Adobe has added Google Analytics to these released documents to make it easier to track traffic and activity.

**This is an easy guide on how to use the Publish Online tool and connect to Google Analytics:**

## Accessing the Publish Online Function

1. Open your InDesign document.
2. Click on the "File" menu.
3. Choose "Publish Online" from the list of options.

## Integrating Google Analytics

- In the Publish Online dialog box, look for the options that have to do with tracking or analytics metrics.
- You can now add Google Analytics to your released documents using Adobe InDesign. By keeping track of data like page views, user conversations, and more, this integration lets you learn a lot about how well your digital publications are doing.
- Make sure you have the tracking code and a Google Analytics account.
- In the Publish Online settings, enter the necessary Google Analytics tracking information. This usually has your Google Analytics Tracking ID in it.
- Once you have entered all the necessary information, share your document online.

This function is also impressive because it lets you find text in your published documents. Users can quickly and easily find the information they need from any device thanks to this feature. But it's important to know that touch devices are the only ones that can do text finding right now.

## Key Features

1. **Text Search on Touch Screens**:
   - Users can use touch devices to do text searches right inside published documents.
   - This feature is especially helpful for people who use phones or tablets because it makes it easy to find specific information in the content.
2. **Copy Text on Desktop and Laptop Devices:**
   - People who use desktops and laptops have an extra benefit besides text finding. They can look for text in published documents and copy it as well.
   - This extra feature makes standard computers easier to use by letting users get information and use it without any problems.

**How to Utilize:**

- People who use touch devices only need to start the text search function in the published document interface.
- Laptop and desktop users cannot only look for text, but they can also use the copy function to get the information they've found and use it. Users who need to move information from the published document to other programs or documents will benefit the most from this new feature.

These improvements to text search are in line with Adobe's goal of making the software flexible and easy to use on a wide range of devices. Including these features makes sure that users can easily connect with and get information from released documents, meeting the needs of both authors and readers.

# Harfbuzz

The addition of Harfbuzz as the default shape engine in World Ready Composer is one of the most important changes. This is a big improvement to InDesign's shape engine, which will help people who work with complicated forms from African and Indian languages.

## Key Features of Harfbuzz Integration

1. **Enhanced Shaping and Rendering:**
   - Users can expect a big improvement in the shaping and display of images when Harfbuzz is set as the default shaping engine. This is especially true for languages from the Indic and MENA regions.
   - The integration makes sure that signs are displayed more precisely on screens and in print, which helps make the design more accurately represented.
2. **Support for Complex Scripts:**
   - Harfbuzz is intended to handle intricate writing with ease, and the fact that it is integrated into InDesign makes it especially useful for languages like Arabic, Hebrew, Hindi, and others.
   - Designers who work with these complicated scripts can now enjoy text that is rendered more smoothly and accurately, which makes the design process go more smoothly and reliably.
3. **Improved World Ready Composer:**
   - Harfbuzz adds to the features of InDesign's World Ready Composer, making it even better at working with a wide range of scripts and languages.
   - With these changes, users can make content that fits the subtleties and complexities of languages that need complex shapes and rendering.

## User Experience and Precision

- The clarity and correctness of displaying glyphs in InDesign will get a lot better for designers working on projects that use Arabic, Hebrew, Hindi, and other languages.
- The improved shape engine makes the user experience better by making sure that the representation of text visually matches the design exactly, both on screens and in printed materials.

In conclusion, making Harfbuzz the default shape engine in Adobe InDesign is a big step forward for helping designers who work with complicated scripts. This update shows that Adobe is still dedicated to making tools that can be used by people all over the world. It makes the writing experience better for a wider range of languages and scripts.

# UXP Plugins

The launch of UXP (Unified Extensibility Platform) plugins was one of Adobe MAX's most notable developments. Because they make work easier and faster, plugins are very important in the design and marketing worlds. It's a big deal that UXP is now available because it lets developers use current JavaScript features to make tools for Adobe InDesign and other Creative Cloud PC apps.

## Key Features and Advancements with UXP Plugins

1. **Modern JavaScript Capabilities:**
   - UXP plugins let developers use the newest features and functions of current JavaScript. So, writers can use the most recent language features to make plugins that work well and are strong.
2. **Customization of InDesign Experience:**
   - UXP plugins let users change how they use InDesign by adding new tools, incorporating automated tasks, and making their user interfaces.
   - At this level of customization, users can make their workspace fit their needs, which makes the whole process much more efficient and users happier.
3. **Empowered Development with JavaScript, HTML, and CSS:**
   - The addition of UXP lets developers use their knowledge of JavaScript, HTML, and CSS to make plugins.
   - This well-known and widely-used web development stack makes it easy for developers to use their skills to make unique solutions for InDesign. This makes the development environment more open and available to everyone.
4. **Enhanced Workflows:**
   - UXP plugins are very important for improving processes because they add custom solutions. Users can now make their work easier by automating jobs they do over and over again and adding new tools straight to the InDesign environment.
   - This makes the workspace more efficient and dynamic, so marketers and designers can spend more time being creative and less time doing boring and manual time-consuming tasks.

## Empowering Creativity with UXP Plugins

- The release of UXP plugins shows Adobe's dedication to encouraging creation by giving developers premium tools to improve and expand the features of InDesign and other Creative Cloud apps.
- By providing a platform that works well with current web development methods, Adobe creates a community where developers can work together and share new ideas, which eventually helps the design and publishing community as a whole.

# System Requirements

**The following are the system requirements for Adobe InDesign:**

- **Developer:** Adobe Inc.
- **Operating System:**
  - Microsoft Windows 7 with Service Pack 1, Windows 8, Windows 8.1, or Windows 10
- **Processor:**
  - Intel Pentium 4 or AMD Athlon 64 processor
- **Touch Workspace:**
  - To utilize the new InDesign Touch workspace, a touchscreen-enabled tablet/monitor running Windows 8 or above is required.
- **RAM (Memory):**
  - 4 GB of RAM (16 GB recommended)
- **Hard Disk Space:**
  - 2.6 GB of available hard disk space for installation
  - Additional free space is required during installation. Note that installation on removable flash storage devices is not supported.

- **Display:**
    - 1024 x 768 display (1280 x 800 recommended) with 32-bit video card
    - Supports HiDPI display for enhanced resolution
- **Adobe Flash Player:**
    - Adobe Flash Player 10 software is required to export SWF files.

People who want to run Adobe InDesign on their Windows computers can use these system needs as a starting point. Going above and beyond the suggested system requirements, especially when it comes to RAM and screen quality, can improve the general speed and user experience when using InDesign, especially for jobs that require a lot of graphics. Also, the fact that Adobe Flash Player is mentioned brings attention to its role in certain exporting functions for SWF files.

# How to update your Adobe InDesign

**Step 1:** On your computer, open the **Creative Cloud** desktop app. From the menu on the left, choose **Apps**.

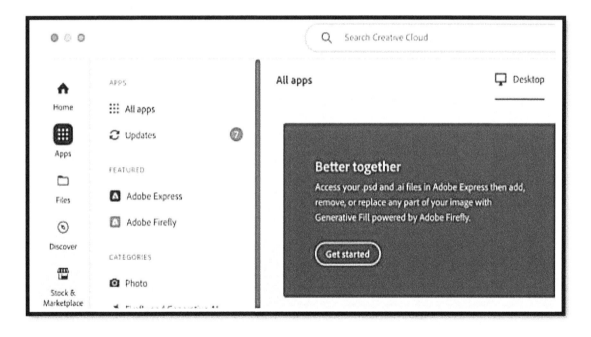

**Step 2:** Below the title **"Installed,"** you should see three columns. What should be in the middle column? It should say either **Update Available** or **Up to date**. Click on the **"Update Available"** button next to "InDesign." It will take you to a new screen with a list of all the updates for the apps.

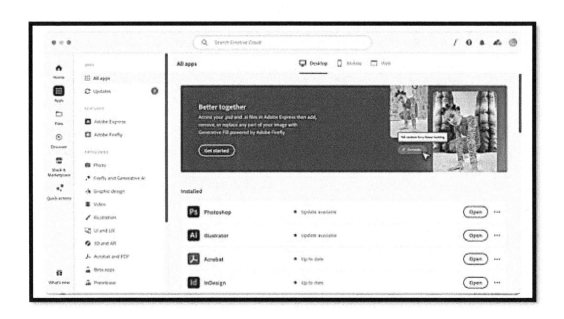

To get to the list of apps that need to be updated, you can also click **Updates** in the window that runs across the left. After you click **"Update,"** wait for the app to finish installing.

# CHAPTER 2
# SETTING UP YOUR WORKSPACE

## Workspace Overview

Some of the Adobe Creative Cloud apps, like InDesign, have user interface features like panels, bars, and windows that make it easier to create and handle documents. The way these things are set up and arranged together makes up what is called a "workspace." Workspaces give users a planned and well-organized place to quickly find their way around an app's features and tools. The goal is to improve user efficiency and make processes more efficient.

## Key Elements of Workspaces

1. **Panels, Bars, and Windows:** Workspaces are made up of important interface elements like panels, bars, and windows that are arranged in a way that helps with different program tasks and functions.
2. **Consistent Appearance:** Workspaces have the same look, so they are all the same in different parts of the program. This choice in design makes things easier for the user and makes it simple to switch between tasks or functions.
3. **Customization Options:** Users can change their workspaces to fit their tastes and ways of working. This customization can include moving panels around, changing the layout, or making some parts less or more visible.

## Home Screen

When you open InDesign for the first time or when there are no documents open, the Home screen is the first thing that you see. It gives users quick access to important features like tutorials, options for creating documents, and the ability to open projects that have already been saved.

## Customization

- Users can modify their workspace by choosing from pre-set options made for specific tasks or by making their unique setups. Individuals can tailor their surroundings to their particular wants and working styles thanks to their flexibility.

**These tabs and buttons are on the Home screen:**

| | |
|---|---|
| **New file:** | To create a new document, click this button. One of the many templates and presets that are available in InDesign can be used to create a document. |
| **Open:** | Click this button to open an existing document in InDesign. |
| **Home:** | Click this tab to see the most recent changes you made to files. |
| **Learn:** | InDesign lessons for beginners and experts can be found on this tab. Clicking on it will bring up a list of courses. |

**Note:** To turn off the Home screen in the **Preferences** menu, go to **Preferences** > **General** and uncheck the box next to **Show Home Screen When No Documents Are Open**. It is still possible to use the keyboard keys Ctrl/Cmd + O and Ctrl/Cmd + N.

# Workspace overview

InDesign's workspace lets you change how the windows, panels, and tools are laid out, so you can make your own unique design area.

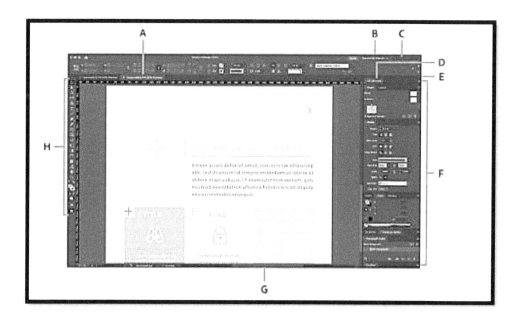

**A.** Tabbed Document windows **B.** Workspace switcher **C.** Search bar with autocomplete suggestions **D.** Panel title bar **E.** Collapse to Icons button **F.** Panel groups in vertical dock **G.** Status bar **H.** Tools panel

## Application Frame

- The Application frame is a window that connects all the parts of the Adobe InDesign area so that they work well together as a single unit. The design of this frame keeps things from clashing, and it can be adjusted quickly when the size or position is changed. Panels inside the Application frame can be seen even when you switch to or click on something outside of the application. People who are working with more than one program can put them next to each other or on different computers. Through the Window menu on macOS, you can turn on or off the standard user interface.

## Application Bar

- The desktop switcher, menus (only in Windows), and other program settings are in the Application bar, which runs across the top. When the Application frame is off on macOS, you can get to the application bar. The Window menu gives users the freedom to turn it on or off as needed.

## Tools Panel

- The Tools panel is an important part that has many tools for making and editing pictures, artwork, and page elements. The functionality of the tools is used to organize them sensibly, making them easier to find and more efficient for users.

## Control Panel

- The Control panel shows options that are related to the currently chosen item, making it easy for users to get to the setup settings. This makes updating easier by making sure that the right options are always close at hand.

## Document Window

- The Document window is where the user works with the file most of the time. It shows what's in the text and can have windows that are grouped or sorted. Document windows can be grouped and docked in some situations to make them easier to find.

## Panels

- Adobe InDesign's panels are a great way to keep an eye on work and make changes to it. Users can arrange them in any way they like—grouped, stacked, or docked. Panels make it easier to get to different functions, tools, and information, which make the area more efficient overall.

# Change screen modes

To change how visible the document window is, go to **View > Screen Mode.** When the toolbar is in a single column, click the "current mode" button to get to the menu where you can pick from different modes.

| | | |
|---|---|---|
| **Normal Mode:** | | Shows artwork in a normal window with all lines and guides visible, as well as items that aren't being printed and a white board. |
| **Preview Mode:** | | Shows artwork as if it were printed, hiding all parts that aren't needed for printing (like grids, guides, and objects that aren't needed for printing) and setting the pasteboard's background color to the preview color set in Preferences |
| **Bleed Mode:** | | This mode shows the artwork as if it were printed, hiding any elements that aren't needed for printing (like grids, guides, and objects that aren't needed for printing). The |

pasteboard is set to the preview background color chosen in Preferences, and any printing elements within the document's bleed area (set in Document Setup) are shown.

**Slug    Mode:**    In slug mode, it displays artwork as if it were printed with all non-printing elements (like grids, guides, and non-printing objects) hidden, the pasteboard is set to the preview background color set in Preferences, and any printing elements within the document's slug area (set in Document Setup) are shown.

**Presentation    Mode:**    This mode shows the artwork as if it were a slideshow presentation, with no choices, panels, or tools visible.

# Use the status bar

In Adobe InDesign, the progress bar in the lower-left corner of the document window is useful for getting information about the file and making it easier to move between pages. Users can use its menu to do different things, which makes their work easier and helps them keep track of their files.

## Menu Options

1. **Reveal in File System (Windows) or Finder (macOS):**
   - On Windows, you can use the "Reveal in Explorer" option in the status bar menu to show the file in the file system.
   - The same thing can be done on macOS by pressing "Reveal in Finder." This option starts the Finder and shows where the file is stored in the file system.

2. **Reveal in Adobe Bridge:**
   - To open Adobe Bridge and find the file, users can choose "Reveal in Bridge" from the menu in the status bar. This option makes it easier to integrate with Adobe Bridge so that you can handle your files better.

## Note on Zoom Percentage Display

- On macOS, users can show the zoom percentage in the status bar by removing the application bar. The "Application Bar" can be turned on and off by going to the "Window" menu and picking "Application Bar."
- However, Windows users can't hide the application bar in Adobe InDesign like macOS users can.

All of these menu options and extra features make the Adobe InDesign experience more complete and easier to use. They make it easier to handle files, move between pages, and change how they see things based on their operating system.

# Control panel overview

The Control panel, which you can get to by going to Window > Control, is a flexible and adaptable tool in Adobe InDesign that makes it easy to get to options, instructions, and related panels for certain page items. The Control panel is initially docked at the top, but users can change its location by docking it at the bottom, turning it into a moving panel, or hiding it completely.

## Key Features and Options

1. **Frames:** The Control panel's option to scale, move, tilt, spin, or apply object styles is available when working with frames. This gives you a central place to change different frame characteristics within the text.
2. **Text:** The Control panel shows word or phrase options for text-related choices. To quickly switch between these options, users can click on the items on the left side of the Control panel. This makes it easier to change the characteristics of text based on certain needs.
3. **Tables:** The Control panel has options to change the size, join rows, arrange text, and add lines when working with tables. This specific set of tools makes it easy to customize tables, which improves the user experience when working with tabular material.

## Tooltips and Additional Information

- Additionally, users can get more information about each option in the Control panel by using Tooltips. This is because the options change depending on what is chosen. Tooltips are short instructions that show up when you move the finger over an icon or option name. This function helps give people relevant knowledge and direction.

## Opening Dialog Boxes

- The Alt + Click (Windows) or Option + Click (macOS) keyboard shortcut can be used to open dialog boxes that are linked to Control panel buttons. The quick switch to thorough settings and setups for certain options is made possible by this feature.

The flexible and context-aware options in the Control panel, along with its combination with Tooltips, make Adobe InDesign's design environment more efficient and easier to use. Because it puts settings for different page features in one place, it makes the work flow smoother and makes design tasks easier and more accurate.

Control panel with tool tip displayed

# Workspace Configuration

## Managing Windows and Panels in Adobe InDesign

For a customizable and streamlined Adobe InDesign process, you need to be able to manage document windows and panels well. You are free to make your own work spaces, move windows, and change the way panels look however you like. You can also save these personalized workspaces so they are easy to get to when you need them.

## Creating Custom Workspaces

1. **Customizing Windows:**
   - Move and change the positions of document windows to make a layout that works for you.
   - Open more than one file at once. If the Document windows are tabbed, you can move them around by dragging the tab of one window to a different spot in the group.
2. **Docking Document Windows:** Docking includes putting Document windows in a group. To move a window into a different group of Document windows, just drag it into the group you want.
3. **Undocking (Floating or Untabbing) Document Windows:** By dragging the tab of a Document window out of the group, you can undock the window from the group. This lets the window move on its own or stops being linked.

## Saving Custom Workspaces

- Once you've set up the document windows and screens the way you want, you can save the custom workspace to use again later.

- Go to Window > Workspace > New Workspace to save a workspace. Give your custom workspace a name and pick which parts of it to include, like document windows, menu arrangements, and so on. To save, click OK.

## Switching Between Workspaces

- The unique workspaces you've saved can be easily switched between once you've saved them. Select the Workspace you want from the list by going to Window > Workspace.

You can change your Adobe InDesign workspace to fit your tasks and tastes if you learn how to handle windows and panels in this way. This level of customizing makes you more productive by making sure that the documents and tools you need are easy to find and set up in a way that fits your routine.

# Dock and undock panels

When you use Adobe InDesign, a dock is a group of panels or panel groups that are shown together, usually vertically. Users can make their workspace fit their needs by docking and undocking panels.

**This makes it easy to get to the tools and functions they need. This is how you can manage panels in a dock:**

- **Docking a Panel:** To dock a single panel, grab it by its tab and drag it to where you want it to be. Docks can be put between panels, at the top, or the bottom.
- **Docking a Panel Group:** Panel groups with multiple tabs can be docked by dragging the full group into the dock using the title bar (the solid, empty bar above the tabs).
- **Removing a Panel or Panel Group:** When you want to get rid of a panel or panel group from the dock, drag it out by its tab or title bar. You can let it float on its own or move it to a different dock by doing this.
- **Customization Tips:** You can move panels around in a dock to make it work better for you. For instance, putting together pieces that do the same thing can make them work better.

## Overall Steps

1. **Docking a Panel:**
   - First, grab it by its tab.
   - Drag it to where you want it to dock (at the top, bottom, or between other panels).
2. **Docking a Panel Group:**
   - Grab the title bar of the whole panel group.
   - Move the group to the dock by dragging it there.

3. **Removing a Panel or Panel Group:**
   - Drag it out of the dock by its tab or title bar.
   - You can let it float on its own or drop it into another dock.

## Hide or show all panels

- Press **Tab** to show or hide all panels, even the **Tools** and **Control** panels.
- Press **Shift+Tab** to show or hide all windows except the **Tools** and **Control** panels.

## Add, remove, and move panels

**If you take away all of a dock's panels, the dock goes away. By moving panels to the right edge of the workspace until a drop zone shows up, you can make a dock.**

- If you want to add a panel, choose it from the **Window** menu and put it where you want it.
- To get rid of a panel, **right-click** on its tab (Windows) or **control-click** on it (macOS) and choose **Close.**
- Drag a panel by its tab to move it.
- Drag the title bar to move a panel group.

**Note:** The drop zone is activated by where the mouse is placed, not where the panel is placed. If you can't see the drop zone, try moving the mouse to where it should be.

## Stack floating panels

A panel floats easily when you drag it out of its dock, but it doesn't go into a drop zone. With the floating panel, you can put it anywhere in the workspace. You can stack floating panels or groups of panels so that when you drag the title bar at the top, they move together.

- Drag a panel by its tab to the drop zone at the bottom of another panel to stack them.
- Drag a panel up or down by its tab to change how it stacks.

## Collapse and expand panel icons

To make the workspace less crowded, you can shrink panels to icons. Some of the time, windows are folded into icons in the default workspace.

- Click the ≫ button at the top of the dock to make all the panel icons in a column collapse or expand. To make an icon in a single panel bigger, pick it.
- Change the width of the dock to change the size of panel buttons and hide titles for a cleaner look. Expand the dock to see the words on the icons.
- You can move panel icons around in the dock, between docks, or as floating icons by dragging them.

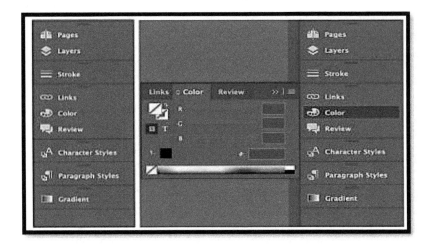

# Scale the user interface

InDesign's **User Interface Scaling** can be changed to fit your needs. When you open InDesign with new preferences, it figures out what size screen you have and changes the application's scaling factor to fit.

**These steps will help you change the size of the user interface on your screen:**

1. For Windows, go to **Edit > Preferences > User Interface**. For macOS, go to **InDesign > Preferences > User Interface**.
2. Choose the **UI Sizing** slider to change the UI's size based on your screen resolution.

There is a sample of the scaled UI next to the slider that you can look at.

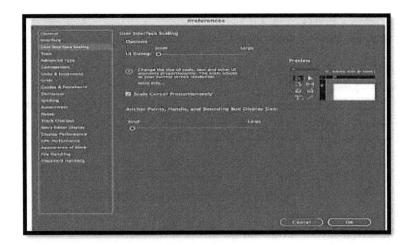

1. Choose the **Scale Cursor Proportionately** option to make the cursor buttons the right size

for the screen.

2. Use the slider to change the size of the **Anchor Points**, the **handle**, and the **Box Bounding Display Size**.
3. Startup InDesign again to use the new settings. The changes will be made the next time you open InDesign, even if you don't restart it now.

# Create and switch workspaces

You can easily get back to the current panel size and position by making a named workspace and saving it. This works even if panels are closed or moved. The workspace switcher in the application bar shows the names of saved workspaces.

1. Go to **Window** > **Workspace** > **New Workspace** and give the workspace a name.
2. Pick one or more of the following options under **Capture**:
   - **Panel Locations:** This item saves where the panels are now (currently).
   - **Menu Customization:** It saves the current set of menus.

## Reset and delete workspaces

- To change a workspace, go to **Windows** > **Workspace** > **Reset** <Workspace name>.
- Go to **Windows** > **Workspace** > **Delete Workspace** to get rid of a workspace.

## Toolbox overview

You can choose, change, and make new page parts with some of the tools in the toolbox. You can pick out types, forms, lines, and colors with other tools. You can change how the toolbox is laid out overall to suit how you like your windows and panels to be set up. By default, the toolbox shows up as a single set of tools going up and down. On top of that, you can make it into a double column or a single row. However, you can't change where different tools are located in the toolbox. You can move the toolbox by dragging its top. Click on a tool in the default toolbox to choose it.

There are also some hidden tools in the toolbox that are tied to the ones that can be seen. Arrows to the right of the tool buttons show you which tools are hidden. To get to a hidden tool, click and hold the tool you want to use in the toolbox, and then pick out the hidden tool. When you move the mouse over a tool, the name of the tool and its keyboard shortcut shows up. This text is called the "tool tip." You can disable tooltips by picking "None" from the ToolTips menu in the Interface settings. **Note:** To see what shortcuts and control keys work with the chosen tool, go to **Window** > **Utilities** > **Tool Hints** and open the Tool Hints panel.

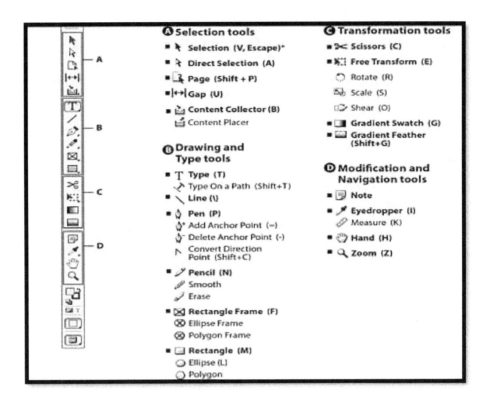

- **Display the toolbox:** Go to Window > Tools.
- **Display tool options:** First, double-click a tool in the list of tools.
- The Eyedropper, Pencil, and Polygon tools are some of the tools that this procedure works for.

## Display and select hidden tools

1. Place the mouse over a tool in the toolbox that has secret tools and hold down the mouse button.
2. Pick a tool when the hidden tools show up.

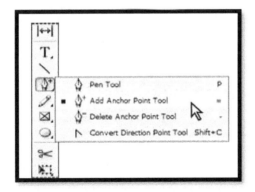

# Select tools temporarily

1. First, choose a tool and hold down the shortcut key for a different tool.
2. Perform an action while holding down the keyboard shortcut.
3. Let go of the keyboard shortcut to go back to the previous tool.

For instance, hold down the V key while the Gap tool is chosen to use the Selection tool for a short time. The Gap tool is chosen when you let go of the V key.

# View tool hints

**The Tool Hints panel tells you how to use the modifier keys with the current tool.**

1. To see the Tool Hints panel, go to **Window** > **Utilities** > **Tool Hints**.
2. Click on a tool in the toolbox to see a list of its modifier keys and methods to use it.

# Change the toolbox layout

1. To change the interface, go to **Edit** > **Preferences** > **Interface** (Windows) or **InDesign** > **Preferences** > **Interface** (Mac OS).
2. From the menu in the Floating Tools Panel, pick a layout option and click OK.

To change how the toolbox is laid out, you can also click the double arrow icon at the top of it.

# Preferences and Settings

Adjusting preferences in Adobe InDesign is a crucial step in tailoring the software to meet your specific needs. Let's delve into the process of customizing general preferences for an enhanced **user experience**

1. **Accessing Preferences:**
   - On Windows, navigate to Edit > Preferences > General.
   - On macOS, go to InDesign > Preferences > General, and then choose your desired preference type.
2. **Page Numbering:**
   - Explore the "View" menu under "Page Numbering" to select a preferred method for numbering pages.
3. **Font Downloading and Embedding:**
   - Determine the font subsetting level based on the number of characters in the Font Downloading and Embedding area. This setting influences font options in Print and Export dialog boxes.
4. **Scaling Preferences:**
   - Customize how scaled items are displayed in panels and how the content of scaled frames behaves in the "When Scaling" area.
     - Opt for "Apply to Content" to adjust the point size when resizing a text

frame. When applied to a graphics frame, the image's percentage size changes while the frame's percentage size remains at 100%.

- Choose "Adjust Scaling Percentage" to view the old and new point sizes side by side during text scaling. Scaling a graphics frame alters both the frame and the image's percentage sizes.

5. **Resetting Warning Dialogs:**
   - Click the "Reset All Warning Dialogs" button to reset all warnings, including those previously marked not to show. This ensures that all warnings are visible, allowing you to make informed decisions about each one.

By configuring these general preferences, you can streamline your workflow and make Adobe InDesign align more closely with your specific requirements. These adjustments pave the way for a more personalized and efficient design experience.

## Document preview

**In Windows' File Explorer and macOS' Finder, you can see previews of your InDesign documents. Not able to see the preview? To add or change the preview settings, do these things:**

1. **Accessing File Handling Preferences:**
   - On Windows, navigate to Edit > Preferences > File Handling.
   - On macOS, go to InDesign > Preferences > File Handling.
2. **Always Save Preview Images with Documents:**
   - Mark the checkbox labeled "Always Save Preview Images with Documents." This ensures that preview images are consistently saved along with your documents.
3. **Choosing Test Settings:**
   - Under the Test Settings section, make selections based on your preferences:
     - **Pages:** Choose from options like First Page, First 2 Pages, First 5 Pages, First 10 Pages, or All Pages to specify which pages you want to save as previews. The default is usually the First 2 Pages.
     - **Preview Size:** Opt for Small (128x128), Medium (256x256), Large (512x512), or Extra Large (1024x1024) to determine the size of the preview image. The default is often Large (512x512).
4. **Applying Changes:**
   - Click the OK button to confirm and apply the selected file handling preferences.

# Customize user interface scaling

Set up InDesign's scaling options so that the user interface is always the same size no matter what your screen resolution is. Some parts of the user interface are scaled correctly so that they look good on high-resolution devices. Once you open InDesign with new preferences, it figures out what size screen you have and changes the app's UI scale to fit. **Note:** Keep in mind that UI scaling doesn't work on low-resolution screens.

Adjusting the user interface scaling in Adobe InDesign can greatly enhance your workspace experience. Here's a simple guide on how to set the user interface scaling:

1. **For Windows Users:**
   - Navigate to Edit > Preferences > User Interface Scaling.
2. **For Mac Users:**
   - Go to InDesign > Preferences > User Interface Scaling.

To change how the Interface looks, use the following options in the User Interface Scaling dialog:

- **UI:** Use the UI size slider to change how big or small the UI is. Most of the time monitors with a better resolution need a bigger scale factor. Next to the tool is a sample of the UI that has been adjusted. To use the new settings, restart InDesign. If you decide to restart later, the changes you made will show up the next time you open InDesign.
  How many stops are shown in the slider depends on the resolution of your screen. For screens with better resolutions, more stops are shown.
- **Cursor:** This option makes the cursor icons the same size as the UI when it is turned on (ON by default).
- **Anchor Points, Handle, and Bounding Box Display Size:** This section lets you change the size of the anchor points, direction handles, and bounding box displays. To do this, move the slider to change the size of the displays.

## Set defaults

If you make changes to the settings while no documents are open, those changes will be used for all new documents. If you make changes while a document is open, those changes will only affect that document. In the same way, if you change settings while no objects are chosen, the new objects will use those values by default.

## Change default settings for new documents

1. **Close All Documents:**
   - Ensure that all open documents are closed before making any changes.
2. **Customize Menu Items, Panels, or Dialog Boxes:**
   - Make the desired modifications to menu items, panels, or dialog boxes based on your preferences.
   - Explore different settings and layouts to tailor the workspace to your specific needs.

**Note**: If your documents share similar characteristics (size and language), you can make these changes even when no document is open.

**For example:**

- To set the usual page size, close all documents, go to File > Document Setup, and select your preferred page size.
- For language preferences, close all documents, navigate to Edit > Preferences > Dictionary (Windows) or InDesign > Preferences > Dictionary (macOS), and choose an option from the Language menu to set the usual dictionary.

By customizing these defaults, you can create a personalized and efficient workspace in Adobe InDesign, enhancing your overall user experience.

## Specify default settings for new objects in a document

1. **Open the Document:**
   - Launch Adobe InDesign and open the document you want to work on.
2. **Deselect All:**
   - Go to the "Edit" menu and select "Deselect All" to ensure that no specific elements or objects are currently selected.
3. **Customize Menu Items, Panels, or Dialog Boxes:**
   - Make the desired changes to menu items, panels, or dialog boxes according to your preferences.
   - Explore different settings and layouts to tailor the document workspace to your specific needs.

## Restore all preferences and default settings

It often fixes problems with InDesign by deleting preferences, which is also called "trashing preferences" or "removing preferences." You should make a copy of the selection files called InDesign Defaults and InDesign SavedData just in case. You don't have to delete your preferences; you can just put these backup files over the corrupted preference files and not lose any of your changes.

**Follow these steps based on your OS:**

**Windows:**

1. Open InDesign.
2. Simultaneously press **Shift + Ctrl + Alt.**
3. Confirm that you want to delete preference files when prompted by clicking "Yes."

**MacOS:**

1. Start InDesign.
2. Hold down **Shift + Option + Command + Control.**
3. Confirm the deletion of preference files by clicking "Yes" when prompted.

# Locating Preference Files

The Adobe InDesign preference files store various program settings and choices. These files, along with the "InDesign Defaults" file, are saved upon closing InDesign. **To manually delete or rename them, navigate to the following directories:**

- **For Windows:**
  - **C:\Users\[username]\AppData\Roaming\Adobe\InDesign\[#]\[language]\**
- **For macOS:**
  - **/Users/[username]/Library/Preferences/Adobe InDesign/[#]/[language]/**

Replace **[username]** with your actual username, **[#]** with the version number (e.g., 15.0 or 14.0), and **[language]** with your language code (e.g., en_US or jp_JP). This process helps reset preferences, potentially resolving issues and enhancing the performance of Adobe InDesign. **Note:** Change [#] to the version number of the product, such as 15.0 or 14.0. Change [language] to the language you want to use, such as en_US or jp_JP.

# CHAPTER 3
# BASIC DOCUMENT CREATION

## Creating a New Document

When you use InDesign to create a document, you don't have to start with a fresh blank document. Instead, you can pick from a lot of different templates, some of which come from Adobe Stock. There are tools in templates that you can use to finish your project. You can work on a template in InDesign the same way you work on any other Adobe InDesign file. Besides using templates, you can also choose one of InDesign's many presets to start making a page.

## Templates and Presets

### Templates

Templates give you rich, creative content that you can use again and again in your documents. You can get templates from Adobe Stock that come with high-quality pictures and graphics that you can use right in InDesign. After that, you can easily make documents that use the same settings and design by adding to these models. For common jobs like design of business cards or handouts, InDesign also offers blank templates with fixed measurements and settings. They are saved as **.indd** files in InDesign.

### Blank Document Presets

Blank document Presets are new documents that already have the right size and settings. It's easy to design for certain gadget shapes or uses when you use presets. Like, you can use a preset to start creating for the iPad right away. Blank document presets have choices for size, pages, columns, alignment, placement, margins, and gaps that are already set. You can change these choices before using the preset to make a document.

**These sets are what templates and presets are categorized into:**

- **Print**
- **Web**
- **Mobile**

## Access the New Document dialog

1. Launch InDesign
2. Do one of these things:
   - Go to **File** > **New**.
   - In the Start workspace, click **New** or **Start New**.
   - Press the following key combination:

- ○ Cmd+N on a Mac
- ○ Ctrl+N on a PC
- Right-click on the tab for an open document and then select "**New Document**" from the menu that appears.

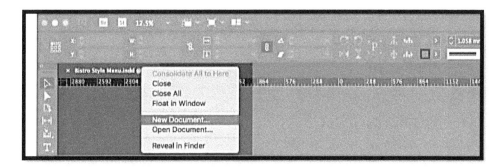

## Overview: New Document dialog

**The New Document dialog box lets you do many things, such as:**

- Create documents using chosen templates from Adobe Stock in several areas, such as **Print**, **Web, and Mobile**;
- Look for more templates on Adobe Stock and make documents using them;
- The **Recent** tab lets you quickly get to files, themes, and other things you've recently used.
- Get to templates you've downloaded from Adobe Stock quickly with the **Saved** tab.
- Use **Blank Document** presets for a variety of groups and device form factors to make documents. You can change the settings for the presets before you open them.

## Create documents using presets

1. In the **New Document** dialog box, click on one of the tabs that say **Print, Web, or Mobile**.
2. Pick out a preset.
3. If you want to, you can change the settings for the preset you chose in the pane on the right called **"Preset Details."**
4. Click on **Create.** The preset tells InDesign to open a new document for you.

## Modify presets

**In the right pane, you can change the settings of a preset document before starting it.**

1. Give the document a name.
2. Choose the following options for the preset that was chosen:

3. Click the **Create** button to start a new document with the preset options.

## Create documents using templates from Stock

There are many templates from Adobe Stock that come with InDesign. There are templates for tablets, phones, letterheads, folders, business cards, and more. Simple fonts or fonts that can be triggered from Adobe Fonts are used in templates with font layers.

**Follow these steps to make a document using a template:**

1. In the New Document window, click on one of the tabs that say **"Print," "Web," or "Mobile."**
2. Pick out a template.
3. Click **"See Preview"** to see what the style will look like. You can look at a sample, which is a picture of a template, and decide if you want to order that template.

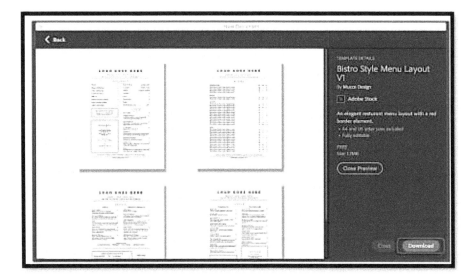

4. Click on **Download**. You are asked by InDesign to buy the template from Adobe Stock. You can open the template as an InDesign file (**.indd**) to work on it after you have licensed it using resources or credits in your account.

5. Click **Open** when the file is done downloading. If you are asked to enable some fonts from Adobe Fonts when you open the template, click **OK**. Right now, you can use InDesign to work on the open file like you would any other **.indd** file.

**Note:** It's important to know that downloaded templates are added to a Creative Cloud library called **Stock Templates**. The **CC Libraries** panel is where you can find this library.

**Note:** InDesign templates have file name extensions that end in **.indt**. But when you open a template, a copy of it is opened as a file with the extension **.indd**. The original **.indt** template doesn't change when changes are made to that **.indd** file.

## Search for more templates from Adobe Stock

Aside from the templates that come with Adobe Stock, you can also use the New Document **window to look for and download many more of these kinds of templates.**

- Click on the **Find More Templates on Adobe Stock** box in the New Document window box and type a search word. On the other hand, you can just click **"Go"** to see all of the possible templates.

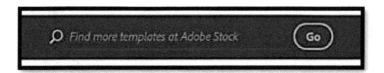

You can look around the Adobe Stock website when InDesign opens it in a new browser window. Choose the one that works best for your project and download it.

## Working with Parent Pages

A parent page, which used to be called a master page, is like a background that you can quickly add to many pages. Things on a parent page show up on all pages that are applied to it. There are dots around parent page things that show up on document pages. When you make changes to a parent page, those changes are instantly made to pages that are linked to it. These pages usually have names, page numbers, heads, and footers that repeat. They can also have blank text or picture frames inside them that look like blank pages in a document. On a document page, you can't choose a parent item unless it is changed. In the realm of digital design, the concept of layers operates much like pages in a document, and understanding their hierarchy is crucial. Imagine layers as transparent sheets stacked on top of each other, akin to pages in a book. **Here are some key insights into working with layers:**

1. **Layer Hierarchy:**
   - Layers can be likened to different pages or levels within a document.
   - Each layer functions as an independent entity, accommodating various elements.
2. **Stacking Order:**
   - Objects within the same layer stack in a specific order. The order is vital because it determines which object appears in front when there is an overlap.
   - When two objects overlap within the same layer, the one placed later in the stacking order will appear in front.
3. **Parent Layers:**
   - Think of parent layers as master sheets that influence the content on document pages.
   - Objects on a parent layer will typically appear behind objects on the document page layer.
4. **Layer Management:**
   - To control the visibility and order of elements, layers can be managed individually.
   - Placing an object on a higher layer means it will appear behind objects on lower layers.
5. **Merging Layers:**
   - Merging layers combines them into a single entity. When this happens, objects on parent layers may be pushed behind those on document page layers.
   - It's essential to consider the layer structure before merging to avoid unintended changes in the stacking order.

Understanding the intricacies of layers is akin to mastering the art of arranging pages in a storybook. Each layer contributes to the overall composition, and manipulating their order can significantly impact the visual narrative of the design.

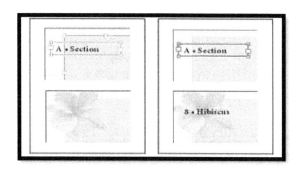

# Tips and guidelines for parent pages

Working with parent layers in your design not only adds versatility but also streamlines your creative process. **Here are some practical tips on harnessing the power of parent layers in your projects:**

1. **Comparing Design Ideas:**
   - Create distinct parent layers and introduce them one by one to sample pages with regular content.
   - This method allows for easy comparison of different design concepts, helping you choose the most effective visual approach.
2. **Document Templates for Efficiency:**
   - Save a set of parent layers in a document template for quick setup of new projects.
   - Your template can encompass color libraries, paragraph styles, character styles, and various presets, ensuring consistency and efficiency across different designs.
3. **Dynamic Layout Adjustments:**
   - Experiment with column and margin settings on parent layers to instantly transform the layout.
   - Adding a new parent layer with different settings dynamically adapts the content on the page, providing a swift way to explore various design possibilities.
4. **Automatic Page Numbers:**
   - When automatic page numbers are applied to a parent layer, they intelligently display the correct page numbers for each section of the document where the parent layer is utilized.
   - This feature enhances document organization and readability, particularly in multi-section projects.

Incorporating these practices into your design workflow empowers you to efficiently iterate through design variations, maintain consistency across projects, and seamlessly adapt layouts for optimal visual impact. Harness the potential of parent layers to elevate the efficiency and creativity of your design process.

## Create parent pages

Understanding the default parent page in every document and its role in creating a cohesive design is crucial. **Here's a breakdown of how parent pages work and how they can simplify your design process:**

1. **Default Parent Page:**
   - Every document is equipped with a default parent page.
   - This default parent serves as the foundation for your document's layout and styling.

2. **Creating New Parents:**
   - Generate new parent pages either from scratch or by deriving them from existing parent or document pages.
   - This flexibility allows you to build upon established designs or start afresh, depending on your project requirements.
3. **Global Changes with Main Parent:**
   - Alterations made to the main parent page automatically propagate to all document pages and other parent pages derived from it.
   - This global synchronization ensures consistency across multiple sections of your document.
4. **Efficient Style Updates:**
   - Planning ahead becomes a powerful strategy, enabling you to modify the style of numerous pages simultaneously.
   - This efficiency is particularly valuable when dealing with extensive documents, saving time and ensuring a unified visual identity.

# Create a parent from scratch

1. **Navigating to the Pages Panel:**
   - To access the Pages panel, begin by opening it and then proceed to the menu section.
2. **Creating a New Parent Object:**
   - Choose "New Parent" from the menu to initialize a new parent object.
3. **Customizing Parent Attributes:**
   - **Input the subsequent particulars and proceed by selecting "OK":**
     - **Prefix:** Offer a succinct prefix consisting of up to four alphanumeric characters, indicating the parent's usage for each page within the Pages panel.
     - **Name:** Allocate a descriptive title to the parent spread.
     - **Based On Parent:** Opt for an existing parent spread as a template for the new parent, or alternatively, opt for "None" to commence from a clean slate.
     - **Number of Pages:** Determine the preferred quantity of pages within the parent spread, with a maximum threshold of ten.

# Create a parent from an existing page or spread

**1. Effortless Transfer Technique:**
- Within the Pages panel, smoothly relocate an entire spread from the Pages section to the Parents section.
- This user-friendly drag-and-drop maneuver promptly converts the chosen spread into a parent, simplifying the organization of your document.

**2. Save As Parent Option:**
- Navigate to the Pages panel and choose a specific spread.
- Opt for the "Save As Parent" option to preserve the selected spread as a designated parent.

- Any objects present on the initial page or spread automatically become integral components of the newly created parent. If the first page utilized a parent, the new parent inherits its foundation.

## Base one parent on another

Within a document, there exists the capability to craft a derivative parent version, influenced by another parent, colloquially known as the "parent parent." The components inherited from the parent parent are aptly labeled as child parents. Envision a scenario where your document comprises ten sections, each utilizing analogous parent spreads. Instead of individually adjusting each section, a more efficient approach involves the creation of a singular parent spread encompassing the shared style and elements present in all ten sections. In this context, effecting a general design modification becomes a streamlined process. A simple adjustment to the parent parent suffices, automatically applying the alterations across all ten sections. This dynamic mirrors the concept of a master template, ensuring uniformity throughout distinct segments of your document. Furthermore, you have the flexibility to customize child parents to suit your preferences. Adjusting the parent items on a child-parent allows you to make changes to the parent, just as you would modify elements on regular document pages. This approach not only maintains a uniform design but also enables you to keep it fresh and updated easily. In the realm of desktop publishing and layout design, Adobe InDesign is a powerful tool with numerous features to enhance efficiency and creativity. One such feature involves manipulating parent spreads within the Pages panel to influence the appearance of certain elements. To make one parent look like another, follow the steps outlined below:

## Method 1: Using the Pages Panel Menu

1. Launch your InDesign document.
2. Find your way to the Pages panel by opting for "Window" in the top menu and then selecting "Pages."
3. Identify the specific parent spread you intend to modify.
4. Open the Pages panel menu by clicking on the menu icon positioned in the top-right corner of the panel.
5. Within the menu, opt for "Parent Options for [parent spread name]." Substitute "[parent spread name]" with the designated name of the parent spread requiring modification.
6. In the ensuing dialog box, pinpoint the "Based On Parent" option.
7. Choose an alternative parent from the array of available options.
8. Confirm the changes by selecting "OK."

## Method 2: Dragging and Dropping

1. Open your InDesign document.
2. Go to the Pages panel by selecting "Window" in the top menu and choosing "Pages."
3. Locate the parent spread you want to use as the base.
4. Click and hold on the parent spread's name.
5. Drag the selected parent spread onto the name of another parent spread.

6. Release the mouse button to drop the parent spread.

# Edit the layout of a parent

In Adobe InDesign, manipulating the style of parent pages is a dynamic process that allows you to implement changes seamlessly across multiple pages in a document. **Here are the steps to change the style of parent pages:**

1. **Access the Parent Page:**
   - Open your InDesign document.
   - Navigate to the Pages panel by selecting "Window" in the top menu and choosing "Pages."
   - Locate the parent page button in the Pages panel.
2. **Double-Click or Choose from List:**
   - Execute a double-click on the parent page button situated within the Pages panel.
   - Alternatively, you have the option to designate the parent page by selecting it from the list of text boxes positioned at the bottom of the document window.
3. **Modify the Parent:**
   - Once the parent spread is displayed in the document box, make the necessary changes to the parent page.
   - You can add or edit text, insert images, adjust layout elements, or apply any other design modifications.
4. **Update Across Pages:**
   - Modifications applied to the parent page resonate across all pages utilizing that specific parent.
   - As an illustration, introducing text or embedding an image on the parent page manifests identical content on all pages linked to that parent.

## Important Note

- It's essential to be aware that if you modify or remove a parent page object on a specific page, that object may not update to reflect changes made on the parent page.
- In other words, if you make local changes to an object on a page, it might not synchronize with the corresponding object on the parent page.

Any pages that use that parent are updated automatically by InDesign. Pick out the parent page with the Page tool, and then use the Control panel's size options to make it a different size. Utilizing multiple views in Adobe InDesign is a valuable technique to observe the effects of changes made to parent pages.

**Here's how you can do it:**

1. **Open Multiple Views:**
   - Navigate to the top menu and select "Window."

- Choose "Arrange" and then select "New Window."
- Once the new window is open, go back to "Window > Arrange" and select "Tile" to arrange the views side by side.

2. **Assign Views to Page and Parent:**
   - In one of the views, navigate to a specific page of your document that uses the parent page.
   - In the other view, navigate to the parent page itself.

3. **Make Changes to the Parent:**
   - In the view displaying the parent page, make the desired changes to the layout, text, or any other elements.

4. **Observe Changes in Page View:**
   - Switch to the view displaying the page associated with the parent.
   - As you make changes to the parent, you will observe real-time updates on the page view.

## Change parent page options

1. **Select the Parent Spread:**
   - Open the Pages panel in Adobe InDesign.
   - Click on the name of the parent spread for which you want to modify the options.

2. **Access Parent Options:**
   - In the Pages panel, click on the menu icon (usually represented by three horizontal lines or a small dropdown arrow).
   - From the menu, choose "Parent Options for [parent name]." This option allows you to access and modify the settings for the selected parent spread.

3. **Modify Options:**
   - Upon initiation, a dialog box materializes, showcasing an array of options pertaining to the parent spread. Feel free to modify any preferred settings, including altering the parent's name or title, selecting an alternative parent for "Based On Parent," or fine-tuning the number of pages within the parent spread as needed.

4. **Apply Changes:**
   - After making the necessary modifications, click "OK" to apply the changes.

# Apply parent pages

If your document incorporates unique layouts, such as a magazine foldout spanning three or four pages, each parent used in this context should consistently have an identical page count. Any deviation in page count may alter the size of the layout page. In cases where the parent page exhibits a distinct page size compared to the layout page, it influences the dimensions of the layout. If the layout page boasts its own customized page size, you have the option to adopt the dimensions of the parent page or maintain the layout page's specific size. It's important to take note that the periphery of parent items within a text page is delineated. There is a possibility that the parent item is concealed on a lower layer or that the parent items are hidden, rendering them imperceptible on the page. To address this, navigate to the Pages panel menu and select "Show Parent Items" to reveal any obscured elements.

## Apply a parent to a document page or spread

1. Grasp the parent page icon and drag it onto the designated page icon within the Pages panel. Release the mouse button when a black rectangle materializes, signifying the selection of the page you intend to link with the parent.
2. Alternatively, if you opt to assign a parent page to an entire spread, access the Pages panel. Subsequently, drag the parent page icon to one of the corners of the spread. Release the mouse button when a black rectangle envelops all the pages within the spread that you aim to associate with the parent.

## Apply a parent to multiple pages

1. **Manual Selection:**
   - Go to the Pages panel and opt for the pages you wish to associate with a new parent.
   - Click on the desired parent while simultaneously holding down Alt (Windows) or Option (Mac OS).
2. **Menu Option:**
   - Navigate to the Pages panel and access the menu.
   - Choose "Apply Parent to Pages" from the menu.
   - Select the parent you want to apply.
   - Verify that the intended page groups are chosen under the "To Pages" option.
   - Confirm the application of the parent to the selected pages by clicking OK.

It's worth noting that multiple pages can share the same parent simultaneously. If you want to apply the same parent to non-consecutive pages, you can use a comma-separated format (e.g., 5, 7-9, 13-16) to specify the pages you wish to include in the parent assignment. These methods provide a convenient way to efficiently manage and apply parent-child relationships to multiple pages in your document.

## Unassign parents from document pages

1. Navigate to the Pages panel and locate the "Parents" section.
2. Within the "Parents" section, select "None" as the parent. This action will effectively unassign any existing parent from the chosen page.

When you remove a parent from a page, it results in the page's style and elements no longer inheriting characteristics from that parent. However, instead of completely unassigning the parent, you have the option to override specific parent items on individual document pages. This enables you to edit or modify these items exclusively on the chosen pages, providing flexibility when you need to retain most of the elements from a parent but wish to make specific alterations on certain pages. This approach allows for efficient customization without losing the overall structure provided by the parent.

# Copy parent pages

1. **Copy from One Document to Another:**
   - Open the document where you want to establish a new parent.
   - Copy the desired parent from another document.
   - Paste the copied parent into the current document, creating a new parent relationship.
2. **Copy Within the Same Document:**
   - If you wish to duplicate a parent within the same document, copy the parent from its source.
   - Paste it onto another parent within the document, effectively creating a new parent based on the copied one.
3. **Copy to Other Documents:**
   - If you have a parent configured in one document and want to use it in others, copy the parent from the source document.
   - Paste the parent into the target document(s), establishing the same parent structure across multiple documents.
4. **Syncing Documents in a Book:**
   - If you are working with a book that contains multiple documents, sync the documents within the book.
   - This synchronization process can bring parent pages from one document into another, facilitating consistency across the entire book.

# Copy a parent within a document

**To replicate a parent spread within your document using the Pages panel, you can employ either of the following techniques:**

1. **New Page Button:**
   - Within the Pages panel, locate and click on the "New Page" button positioned at the panel's bottom.
   - Drag the page name of the desired parent spread to be duplicated and release it onto the newly generated page. This process effectively duplicates the parent spread.
2. **Panel Menu Option:**
   - Identify the page name of the parent spread you intend to duplicate within the Pages panel.
   - Right-click on the page name or access the panel menu.
   - From the available menu options, opt for "Duplicate Parent Spread [spread name]." This action duplicates the parent spread, generating a copy with an adjusted page prefix, typically advancing to the next letter in the alphabet.

Upon copying a parent spread, it's important to note that the page prefix associated with the duplicated parent spread will automatically change to the next letter in the alphabet. These methods provide a straightforward way to replicate parent spreads, maintaining consistency and facilitating efficient page management within your document.

## Copy or move a parent to another document

1. **Open Both Documents:**
   - Open the document where you intend to add the new parent.
   - Simultaneously, open the file that contains the parent you want to copy.
2. **Copy or Move Parent in Source Document:**
   - In the Pages panel of the source document:
   - To duplicate the entire parent spread, click and drag it to the window of the new document.
   - Alternatively, pick the specific parent you wish to copy or relocate.
   - Navigate to "Layout > Pages > Move Parent" in the menu.
   - From the "Move To" menu, designate the document name where you intend to relocate the parent.
   - If the intention is to eliminate the copied pages from the original file, opt for "Delete Pages after Moving," and subsequently click OK.
3. **Address Duplicate Prefix:**
   - In cases where the target document already has a parent with the same prefix, the system automatically assigns the next letter in the alphabet to the moved parent. This ensures unique identification and avoids conflicts.

## Delete a parent from a document

1. **Selecting Parent Page Icons:**
   - Head to the Pages panel.
   - Choose one or more parent page icons slated for deletion.
   - Note: To obtain a list of all parent pages not currently in use, access the Page panel menu and opt for "Select Unused Parents."
2. **Deletion Options:**
   - After selecting the parent page icons, proceed with one of the subsequent deletion methods:
     - Drag the chosen parent page or spread icon onto the "Delete" icon positioned at the base of the Pages panel.
     - Click the "Delete" button located at the panel's bottom.
     - Alternatively, access the panel menu, select "Delete Parent Spread [spread name]," and validate the deletion.

Upon deleting a parent, any page in the document associated with that parent will now have the [None] parent applied instead. This ensures that the document maintains a coherent structure even after the removal of a parent, with affected pages reverting to the default parent setting.

These steps provide a straightforward way to manage and modify parent relationships within your document.

## Override or detach parent items

When you introduce a parent page to a document page, all the elements present on the parent page, known as parent items, automatically appear on the document page. There are instances when you desire a document page to closely resemble a parent page. In such cases, you don't necessarily have to create a new parent or reconstruct the entire parent layout on the document page. Instead, you have the option to modify or eliminate specific parent items from the page, and the remaining parent elements will still update in tandem with the parent.

**It's crucial to recognize that overriding parent items and removing them from a document page are distinct actions:**

- **Overriding Parent Items:**
    - This involves modifying or altering specific parent items on a document page without completely removing them.
    - The overridden items on the document page will maintain their modified state independently of changes made to the parent.
    - This allows for customization on a per-page basis while retaining the overall structure from the parent.
- **Removing Parent Items from a Document Page:**
    - This action entails eliminating specific parent items from a document page entirely.
    - Once removed, the document page will no longer display the removed parent items, and any updates to the parent will not affect these items on the document page.

## Override parent item attributes

When a parent item is overridden on a document page, a duplicated version of the item is placed on the document page while maintaining a connection to the original parent page. This duplicated item, known as the local copy, allows for independent customization without affecting the parent. Following the override of an item, you gain the flexibility to selectively modify the attributes of the local copy to align with your preferences. For instance, you can adjust the fill color of the local copy, and any subsequent alterations to the fill color on the parent page will not affect the local copy. However, attributes such as size will consistently update according to changes made on the parent page unless specifically modified on the local copy. It's crucial to emphasize that the ability to revert to the parent's settings is retained by eliminating overrides. This procedural step ensures synchronization, ensuring that the object on the document page aligns with its parent.

Here are the characteristics you can modify for a parent page object on the document page:

- Strokes
- Fills
- Contents of a frame
- Transformations (rotating, scaling, shearing, resizing)
- Corner options
- Text frame options
- Lock state
- Transparency
- Object effects

# Detach items from their parent

Indeed, the process of separating or detaching a parent item from its parent on a document page is possible. However, certain steps need to be followed:

1. **Override the Parent Item:**
   - Before detaching an item, it must be overridden on the document page, creating a local copy. This local copy becomes independent of the parent's changes.
2. **Detach the Item:**
- Following the override, the item is eligible for detachment or separation from its association with the parent. This operation effectively severs the link between the local copy and the original parent page.

Post-detachment, the local copy of the item on the document page becomes isolated, ceasing to synchronize with any modifications made to the parent page. This independence facilitates distinctive customization, enabling unique adjustments without being influenced by changes applied to the parent.

# Override a parent item

1. **Verify "Allow Parent Item Overrides":**
   - Confirm that the "Allow Parent Item Overrides On Selection" option is activated in the item's Pages panel menu. This setting dictates the permissibility of overriding the parent item.
2. **Override Specific Parent Items:**
   - **To override particular parent items on a document page:**
     - Hold down Ctrl+Shift (Windows) or Command+Shift (Mac OS).
     - Click on the desired item to override (multiple items can be selected by dragging the cursor over them).
     - Modify the selected parent items to your preference. The overridden items can now be treated similarly to any other page items while maintaining linkage to the parent page.

3. **Override All Parent Page Items on a Spread:**
   - **Alternatively, to override all parent page items on a spread:**
     - Select a document spread.
     - From the Pages panel menu, opt for "Override All Parent Page Items."
     - Subsequently, each parent item on the spread can be independently modified.

The change in appearance, from a dotted box to a solid line around a parent item, signifies that a local copy has been generated.

**Note:** When replacing a linked text frame, all frames visible in that thread are also replaced, ensuring consistency in content across linked text frames even if they are on different pages in the spread.

## Detach a parent item

1. **Overwrite the Parent Item:**
   - Press Ctrl+Shift (Windows) or Command+Shift (Mac OS).
   - Click on the specific item on the document page that you want to separate from its parent. This action overwrites the item, creating a local copy.
2. **Detach the Selection from Parent:**
   - After overwriting the item, go to the Pages panel menu.
   - Select "Detach Selection From Parent."

This process disconnects the chosen parent item from its original parent, providing autonomy to the local copy. **If you want to remove all overridden parent items from a spread, use the following steps:**

1. **Select the Spread:**
   - In the document, choose the spread containing the overridden parent items.
2. **Remove Overridden Parent Page Items:**
   - Go to the Pages panel menu.
   - Select "Detach All Objects From Parent."

This action removes all overridden parent items on the selected spread. If the command is unavailable, it indicates that there are no modified items on that spread. These steps offer a precise way to manage the separation of individual parent items or remove all overridden parent items from a specific spread within your document.

## Prevent a parent item from being overridden

**When you need to override all parent items except a few on a document page, you can follow these steps:**

1. **Select the Specific Parent Item:**
   - Pick out the parent item on the parent page that you want to keep unmodified.

2. **Disable Allow Parent Item Overrides On Selection:**
   - In the Pages panel menu, find the item you selected.
   - Uncheck the box that says "Allow Parent Item Overrides on Selection."

By unchecking this option, you prevent modifications to the selected parent item, ensuring it remains unchanged when overriding all other parent items on the document page. When parent items that don't allow modifications are displayed on the page, they have no frame edge, indicating that they are not open to overrides. If you decide to prevent a linked text frame from being overridden, the setting for all text frames in that thread remains consistent across the document.

# Reapply parent items

If you inadvertently override parent elements, there's an option to revert them to their original state on the parent page. This action restores the object's properties to their parent-defined settings, ensuring subsequent updates when the parent is modified. The local copy of the object is removed, and the parent item becomes unselectable due to its bordered marking. You have the flexibility to eliminate modifications for specific objects or for all objects on a spread, although this operation can't be applied to the entire document simultaneously. This nuanced approach allows for targeted adjustments, ensuring precision in restoring or preserving modifications as needed.

1. **Eliminate Overrides on Selected Objects:**

   - Choose the objects originally designated as parent items.
   - Select a spread in the Pages panel.
   - Navigate to the Pages panel menu and opt for "Remove Selected Local Overrides."
   - This action specifically eradicates overrides from the selected objects, allowing for the targeted reversal of particular modifications.

2. **Remove All Overrides from a Spread:**

   - Choose the spread (or parent spread) from which you intend to remove all parent overrides in the Pages panel.
   - Ensure that no items are currently selected by going to Edit > Deselect All.
   - In the Pages panel menu, choose "Remove All Local Overrides."
   - This command globally eliminates all parent overrides within the chosen spread, presenting a comprehensive solution for reverting modifications.

If objects are removed from a parent page, reintegrating them onto the parent page directly is not feasible. However, the option exists to delete the extracted objects and subsequently reinstate the parent onto the page. Upon restoring a parent to a page containing previously overridden parent page objects, the overridden items are expunged, and all parent page objects are reinstated. This process may result in some elements appearing duplicated on the page. To achieve an exact replication of the parent's appearance, it becomes imperative to eliminate the separately modified items.

## Hide parent items

**To conceal parent page items on specific pages in your document, you can utilize the Hide Parent Items tool with the following steps:**

1. **Select Pages to Hide Parent Items:**
   - In the Pages panel, identify and pick the spreads and pages where you wish to hide the parent items.
2. **Activate Hide Parent Items:**
   - Access the Pages panel menu.
   - Choose "Hide Parent Items" from the menu.

By following these steps, the parent items on the selected pages will be hidden, affecting the visual representation and print output of those items. This is useful when you want to temporarily remove certain elements from specific pages without permanently altering the document structure. **To reveal the hidden parent items again, use the following steps:**

1. **Select Spreads to Show Parent Items:**
   - In the Pages panel, select the spreads containing the pages with hidden parent items.
2. **Reveal Hidden Parent Items:**
   - Navigate to the Pages panel menu.
   - Choose "Show Parent Items" from the menu.

These actions allow you to control the visibility of parent items on different pages, providing flexibility in managing the display and output of your document.

## Import a parent from another document

1. **Open Load Parent Pages:**
   - Go to the Pages panel's menu.
   - Select "Load Parent Pages."
2. **Select Source InDesign File:**
   - Locate the InDesign file containing the parent pages you want to import.
   - Double-click on the file to initiate the import process.
3. **Handle Parent Name Conflicts:**
   - **Determine how conflicts with parent names should be resolved:**
     - **Replace Parent Pages:**
       - Choose this option if you want the parents from the source file to replace the parents with the same names in the target file.
       - Safe to use if the target document doesn't have any existing

items with the same names as the incoming parents.

- **Rename Parent Pages:**
  - Opt for this option to change the page names to start with the next letter in the alphabet, avoiding naming conflicts.

When working with parent pages in Adobe InDesign, it's crucial to understand the link established between the source document and the target document upon importing parent pages. **Here's a detailed explanation of how this process works:**

1. **Initial Import and Linking:**
   - Upon the transfer of parent pages from a source document to a target document, an intrinsic connection is established between the modified elements in the target document and their corresponding parent items on the freshly introduced parent pages.
   - This connection guarantees the synchronization of parent pages across different documents, negating the necessity to consolidate these documents into a book.
2. **Ensuring Consistency:**
   - To uphold consistency among parent pages across diverse documents, it is advisable to load the parent pages from the source document before initiating any modifications to objects on the parent pages in the target document.
3. **Management of Overridden Elements:**
   - In instances where overridden items exist in the document (i.e., alterations made to items on the parent pages) without the import of their parents from another source, these overridden items undergo segregation upon the initial loading of parent pages from a source document.
4. **Replacement of Parent Pages:**
   - When introducing parents from a different source document and opting for the replacement of parent pages, the items that underwent modifications in the target document may undergo separation.
   - Any parent pages with matching names in the new source document will be applied to the pages of the target document that contain altered items. This scenario may result in the presence of two sets of objects if not handled with due care.

It's crucial to plan and sequence your actions when working with parent pages, especially when importing them from different source documents. By understanding the link and considering the order of operations, you can effectively maintain consistency and avoid unintended consequences in your InDesign projects.

# CHAPTER 4
# WORKING WITH TEXT
## Adding and Formatting Text

It's time to add information to your document after you've set up its simple layout. Since text is a big part of most InDesign jobs, this is the best place to begin.

There are text boxes in an InDesign document that hold all of the text. You can have as many text boxes of any shape and size as you want. The text boxes can also be linked to each other so that long stretches of text that don't fit in one box will flow into the next linked text box. You can use the **Tools** panel or the keyboard shortcut T to switch to the **Text** tool. To make a text box, click and drag on a blank page. You can now put in the text you want to typeset or use Adobe's famous Lorem Ipsum blank text to fill in the text box. This feature is so useful that Adobe made it a built-in feature.

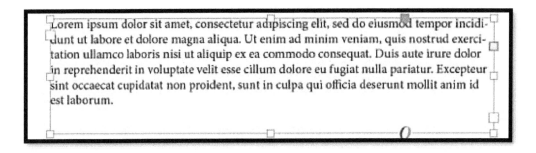

As soon as you click on a text box, the **Control** panel at the top of InDesign will show you different ways to style the text. You can pick the font you want to use and change its size, heading, and other stylistic settings. You can use these settings on whole text boxes or just the part of the text you've chosen, but there's a better way. Instead of formatting each part of your text separately, it's better to use paragraph styles to tag each piece of your text. These styles can then be used again and again. This way, your whole document will look the same, and you won't have to go through each page individually if you need to change the way the text is formatted. You can make a paragraph style for your section headlines, for instance, and then tag each headline with that paragraph style. If you later decide to change how your headlines are formatted, all you have to do is change the settings for the headline paragraph style. All of your headlines will then be formatted in a new way.

When you open InDesign or any other Creative Cloud app from Adobe, a basic set of fonts is already there. However, if you want some new font ideas, you can easily add new fonts. As part of your Creative Cloud account, you can look through the online collection of Adobe Fonts. With just a few clicks, a new font will be linked and ready to use in InDesign.

# Create text frames

In InDesign, text lives in boxes called "text frames." (In QuarkXPress and Adobe PageMaker, a text frame is like a text box and a text block.) Frame grids and plain text frames are the two kinds of text frames. Frame grids are the type of text frames that are only used for writing in Asian languages. They show character emboxes and space as grids. Texts frames that are empty and don't have a grid are called "plain text frames."

**Word and text frames can be moved, resized, and changed, just like graphic frames. What changes you can make depend on the tool you use to choose a text frame:**

- To add or edit text in a frame, use the Type tool $\mathrm{T}$ .
- Use the Selection tool to do general layout work, like putting a frame in the right place and making it the right size.
- To change the shape of a frame, use the Direct Selection tool .
- To make a frame grid, use either the Horizontal Grid tool or the Vertical Grid tool .
- To make a plain text frame for horizontal text, use the Type tool $\mathrm{T}$ . To make a plain text frame for vertical text, use the Vertical Type tool $\mathrm{T}$ . You can change text that is already in a frame with the same tools.

It is also possible to link text frames together so that the text in one frame can move to another frame. When frames are linked in this way, they are called "threaded." A story is a piece of writing that moves through one or more threaded frames. No matter how many frames a word processing file takes up, when you place (import) it, it comes into your document as a single story. Text frames can have more than one column. While text frames can be built on page columns, they can also work without them. That is, a text frame with two columns can fit on a page with four columns. Text frames can be put on parent pages as well, and they can still get text from document pages. **Note:** If you use the same kind of text frame over and over, you can make an object style that has choices for text frames, stroke and fill colors, text wrap and transparency effects, and text frame styling. InDesign adds text frames instantly based on the page's column settings, so you don't have to make them before you place or put text. **A plain text box is made naturally when text is added. You can also manually make a plain text frame that is empty and then type text into it.**

1. **Do any of these things:**
   - Choose the Type tool $\mathrm{T}$ and then drag to set the new text frame's width and height. To make the frame into a square, hold down Shift and drag. When you let go of the

mouse button, a text entry point shows up on the screen.

## Dragging to create new text frame

- Click the in or out port of another text frame with the Selection tool, and then click or drag to make a new frame.
- To put a text file somewhere, use the Place command.
- Click inside any empty frame with the Type tool $\text{T}$ . The empty frame is turned into a text frame if the Type Tool Converts Frames To Text Frames option is chosen in the Type preferences.

## Move and resize text frames

You can move or change the size of text frames with the Selection tool. **Note:** If you want to move or change the size of a text frame without moving from the Type tool $\text{T}$ to a selection tool, hold down Ctrl (Windows) or Command (Mac OS) and drag the frame.

## Move a text frame

- Drag the frame with the Selection tool.
- Hold down Ctrl (Windows) or Command (Mac OS) and drag the frame with the Type tool. The Type tool is still chosen when you let go of the key.

## Resize a text frame

1. **Do any of these things:**
   - Hold down Ctrl (Windows) or Command (Mac OS) and drag any frame handle to change the size of the Type tool $\text{T}$ . The text will be put back together while you change the size of the frame if you hold down the mouse button for one second before you start to drag.

**Note**: If you click on the text frame instead of dragging it, you will lose where you had the text selected or where you had the entry point.

- To change the size of a frame with the Selection tool, drag any of the frame handles on the edge of the frame. To change the size of the words in the frame, hold down Ctrl (Windows) or Command (Mac OS).
- To quickly make the frame fit the text inside it, pick the text frame with the Selection tool and double-click any handle. This will make the bottom of the frame snap to the bottom of the text: double-click the center bottom handle. If you double-click the handle in the middle-right corner, the height stays the same but the width gets smaller to fit the frame.

**TIP:** You can also double-click on a handle on an overset text frame to make the frame wider or taller so that all the text fits inside. If there is more overset text in a text frame than can fit on the page, the text frame is not expanded.

- To make the text frame fit the content, use the Selection tool to pick the frame and then go to **Object** > **Fitting** > **Fit Frame to Content**. The bottom of the text frame is big enough for the text. If there is more overset text in a text frame than can fit on the page, the text frame is not expanded.
- Drag the frame to change its size with the Scale tool .

# Use text frames on parent pages

As soon as you start a new document, you can choose the Primary Text Frame option to put an empty text frame on the document's default parent page. In the New Document window box, the column and border settings were set for this frame.

**If you want to use text frames on parent pages, follow these rules:**

- Use primary text frames when you want a page-sized text frame on every page of your document. You can flow or type your text into these frames. Leave the Primary Text Frame option unchecked and use the Type tool to add text frames to parents if your document needs more variety, like pages with different amounts of frames or frames of different lengths.
- You can add text frames to a parent page to use as placeholders even if you don't choose the Primary Text Frame choice. These empty frames can be put next to each other to make a flow.
- Use the same steps you would use for frames made on document pages to flow text into primary text frames.
- To type text in a document page's primary text frame, hold down Ctrl+Shift (Windows) or Command+Shift (Mac OS) and click on the frame. Then, use the Type tool to click in the frame and start typing.
- Smart Text Reflow can bring in or take out pages automatically as you type or change text. When you type at the end of a linked text frame that is based on a parent page, a new page is added so that you can keep typing in the new text frame. You can change the settings for Smart Text Reflow.
- If you change the page margins, text frames will only change to fit the new margins if the "Enable Layout Adjustment" option is checked.
- If you choose the Primary Text Frame choice, new pages will be added when you autoflow text.

# Paragraph and Character Styles

Open the **Paragraph Styles** window first. Press **F11** or go to **Window** > **Styles** > **Paragraph Styles** if it's not already open. You might find that this opens the **Character Styles** box too. Okay, you'll need it too.

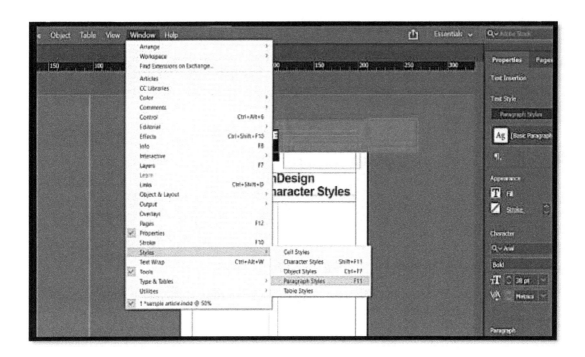

In InDesign, you can put the window anywhere you want. It can be docked on the left or right, but for now, we're going to leave it floating.

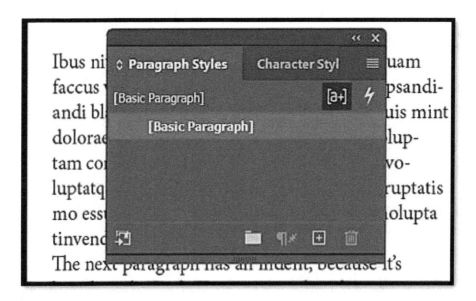

There will already be the [Basic Paragraph] style on your page. Until you choose another style, this is the one that will be used in the new text. You can change this, but not delete it or give it a new name. It will open the Paragraph Styles Options box if you double-click on it.

You can see here how many formatting options are saved in a paragraph style. You can create styles this way, but it's faster to base forms on words that you already have.

First, let's look at a simple two-page document with two headlines, two standfirsts, five subheadings, and some blank text in between the parts. Everything is in the [Basic Paragraph] style at this point.

You can make your first headline look however you want. We picked Arial Black at 30pt for this project. For some reason, the font color is black. You can put your type tool anywhere in the headline text. Click the plus sign at the bottom of the Paragraph Styles box. This will make Paragraph Style 1. If you want to, you can also use the InDesign Story Editor to pick text and change it.

You should name this something more interesting. Left-click the paragraph style name for about half a second and left-click again. You should now be able to change the name of the paragraph style. You can also change the name in the Paragraph Style Options window, which you can get to by clicking on the name of the paragraph style twice.

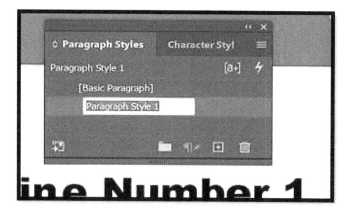

Because we're going to use it for headlines, we named our new paragraph style Headlines. Now, go to the second page and find Main Headline Number 2. Place the mouse anywhere in the headline and choose the Headlines paragraph style that you just set up.

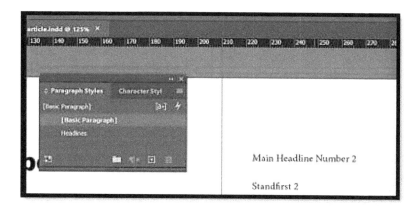

**Right now, this headline looks just like the first one.**

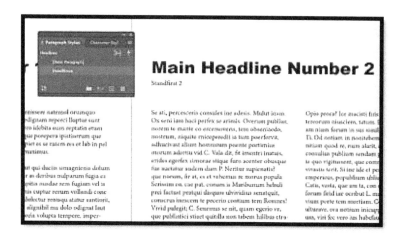

For your standfirsts, follow the same steps, but this time try adding a different color. We chose the color red. This data will be saved by InDesign in both the word and paragraph styles.

Now let's talk about the subheads. We're going to change not only the font and color this time but also the space between the letters (tracking). We'll also make the lines more spaced out (lead), so there will always be a space above the subheads. We have Arial Bold set to 12pt with 23pt Leading and Tracking set to 20 as shown in the picture below. It is also set to blue.

This style can now be used in the rest of your document. You can see how this can save you time when you need to prepare parts of your document that are the same.

# Nested styles and advanced typographic settings

For one or more groups of characters inside a line or paragraph, you can give them different styles. You can even set up two or more stacked styles to work together, with each style picking up where the one before it left off. There is also the option of going back to the first style in the list for paragraphs with layout that is the same and easy to spot. To make run-in headlines look better, nested styles are very useful. For instance, you can use one character style on the first letter of a paragraph and then use a different style that runs through the first colon (:). For each stacked style, you can say which character ends the style. This character could be the end of a word or a tab character.

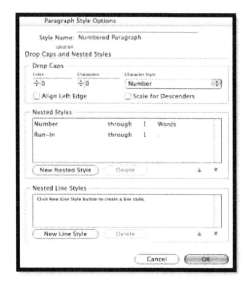

# Create one or more nested styles

**What to do:**

1. One thing you need to do before you can format text is make one or more character styles.
2. **Choose one of the options below:**
   - To add nested styles to a paragraph style, double-click the paragraph style and then click the **Drop Caps and Nested Styles button**.
   - Take a look at the choices in the Paragraph box and choose **Drop Caps and Nested Styles.** This will add nested styles to a single paragraph.

The best results will be achieved by using nested styles as part of paragraph styles. If you apply nested styles to a paragraph as local overrides, changing or formatting changes in the nested style in the future could cause character formatting changes in the styled text that you didn't expect. This could lead to characters being formatted in a way that isn't expected.

3. Choose **"New Nested Style"** and tap it at least once.
4. **Pick one of these choices for each style, then click the OK button:**
   - You can change the way that part of the paragraph looks by clicking on the character style area and then choosing a style from the list that comes up. If you don't already have a character style, select **"New Character Style"** and then describe the formatting you want to use.
   - Please choose the item that ends the formatting of the character style. On top of that, you can type the character, which could be a colon (:) or a specific letter or number.
   - Give the number of times the chosen item has to be used, like the number of lines, words, or sentences that are needed.
   - From the menu, choose either through or Up To. When you choose through, the formatting includes the character that finishes the nested style. But when you choose Up To, the formatting only includes the characters that come before this character.
   - Choose a style and then click either the up▲ or down▼ button to change the order of the styles in the list. The order in which the styles are applied determines the order in which the coding is applied. When the formatting for the first style ends, the formatting for the second style begins. There is an order of styles, and the drop-cap character style is the first one that will work if a style is given to it.

# Loop through nested styles

You can use a series of two or more nested styles in the same paragraph at the same time. One simple way to show this is to change the words in a paragraph from red to green. You could also use nested line styles to make a paragraph with red and green lines that go back and forth. The repeated pattern will stay the same no matter how many words you add or take away from the paragraph.

**These are the steps:**

1. Generate the character types you want to use.
2. Either change a current paragraph style or make a new one. You can also paste the entry point into the paragraph and format it.
3. Choose **New Nested Style** (or **New Nested Line Style**) at least twice in the area or dialog box called Drop Caps and Nested Styles. Then, choose the settings you want for each style.

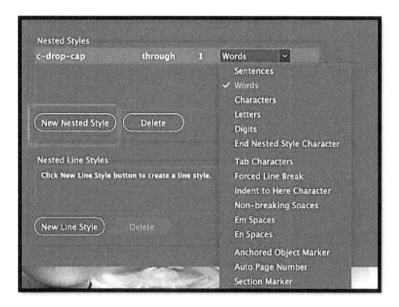

4. **Do any of these things:**
   - In the character style box, select **[Repeat].** Then, click **New Nested Style** a second time to use nested styles. Lastly, you need to set how many nested styles will be used again.
   - After clicking New Nested Line Style a second time, you will need to set the number of lines that will be repeated and then choose [Repeat] from the character style menu.

There are times when you can skip the first style or styles. **"This Week's Events"** might be the first sentence of a paragraph on an events calendar, and then the activities planned for each day of the week would follow. The first nested style would be left out of the loop if you created five nested styles in this case: one for **"This Week's Events,"** one for the day, one for the event, one for the event time, and a final style with a [Repeat] number of three. **"Rcpcat"** should be the last thing on the list. Any style that is placed below the [Repeat] element is not taken into account.

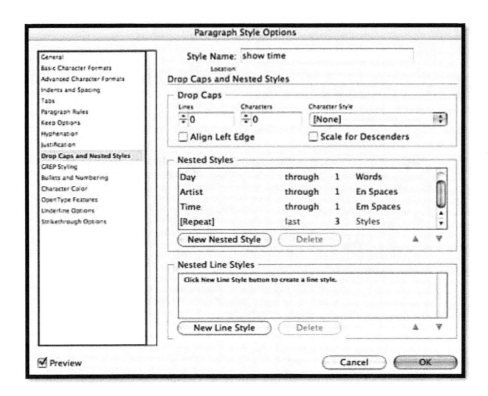

5.  Click the **"OK"** button.

# Text Import and Export

Adding text from different sources to Adobe InDesign is something you will probably have to do a lot when working on print and web design projects. That's possible with InDesign because it works with many file types. You can then add text from many sources.

**Here's how to bring in text from different places:**

1.  Open Adobe InDesign to begin.
2.  You need to either start a new project or open an old one to add text to an existing InDesign document.
3.  Before you add text, you need to make a text frame. To do this, select the **"Type Tool"** from the menu and click and drag on the page to choose where you want the text to go.
4.  You can achieve this by pressing Ctrl + D (Windows) or Cmd + D (Mac), or you can go to **File > Place.**
5.  Find the saved plain text file (TXT) and click on it.
6.  Pick **"Open."**
7.  Choose the same thing, which is **File > Place**.

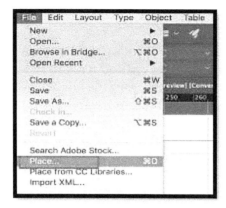

8. Look for the document that Microsoft Word generated and click on it. After that, click **"Open."**
9. If you want to add RTF files along with plain text, you need to follow the steps for adding plain text.
10. InDesign can also bring text straight from PDF files. Select **Place** from the **File** menu to pick out the PDF file.
11. Choose the PDF page or pages that you want to use. After that, click Open.
12. When you add text, you can either link to it or make it part of your document. If you use linked text, any changes you make to the outside file will show up in InDesign. Once the text is integrated, it becomes part of the InDesign document and doesn't need to be linked to a source file.
13. Another box called **"Text Import Options"** might show up after you choose a file. This will let you choose settings like styles, formatting, and more.
14. You can group text frames together if the received text is longer than the first text frame. First, click on the result of the first text frame. Then, click right on top of the second text frame.
15. Check to make sure that the imported formatting, fonts, and special characters are used correctly. If needed, formatting and styles should be changed.
16. If you have linked text, keep track of the files that are linked. If the source files have been changed, you can change the links in InDesign.
17. Once the text is in the document, you should make any last changes you need to the layout, formatting, and styles.
18. To keep all of the changes and import settings, you must remember to save your InDesign document.
19. You can either share or print the document when you're done with your creation.

# Exporting text for collaboration and other applications

**These are the steps:**

1. Open Adobe InDesign first, then the document containing the words you want to export.

2. **Make sure your document's settings are right before you export it. Look at the following things:**
   - **Fonts**: Make sure that the fonts you've chosen can be found on other websites or are embedded on your own. You can add fonts to the document package by going to **"File"** > **"Package"** and then following the on-screen steps. This will let you add fonts.
   - **Images:** When you add pictures to a document, you need to make sure they properly connect. Click **"Window"** and then **"Links"** to see and change photos that are linked.
3. The Text tool can help you choose the text that you want to send. To pick all the words in the document, you can also press the Ctrl+A (Windows) or Command+A (Mac) keys at the same time.
4. After selecting the text, you can copy it to the clipboard by holding down the Ctrl and C keys (Windows) or the Command and C keys (Mac).
5. Open a text editor (like Notepad on Windows or TextEdit on Mac) and press Ctrl+V (Windows) or Command+V (Mac) at the same time to paste the text you copied. Make sure the file ends in .txt when you save it.
6. Should you wish to keep some of the formatting, you can save the text in Rich Text Format (RTF). Start up a text editor, copy and paste the text, and then save the file with the .rtf name.
7. If you want to easily export the whole document while keeping the layout, you should save it as a PDF. Simply go to the **"File"** menu, pick **"Export,"** pick **"PDF"** as the format, make any necessary changes, and then hit **"Export."**
8. To make it easier for people to work together on the project, export the whole InDesign document as an InDesign Markup Language (IDML) file. Go to the **"File"** menu, pick **"Export,"** and choose **"InDesign Markup (IDML)"** as the default format. Then hit **"Save."**

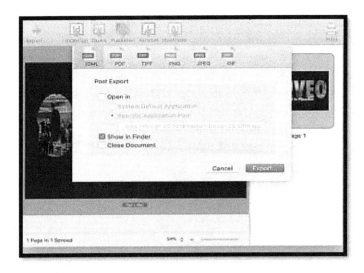

9. Email the exported file to other people, store it in the cloud, or use any other tool that makes working together easier. Make sure the readers have access to the necessary fonts

and files if you plan to share the InDesign document with them.

# Export each story in a different text file (script included in InDesign)

The Adobe team added some tools that you can use to make simple tasks run automatically. There are apps to show you what you can do with a little code in InDesign. There is a script in this group called "Exportallstories" that does exactly what its name says. Double-clicking on "Exportallstories" makes a copy of the text in each story of your document in a text file.

**Here's what you need to do to run the script:**

1. Click on **Window** > **Utilities** > **Scripts** to open the Scripts Panel.

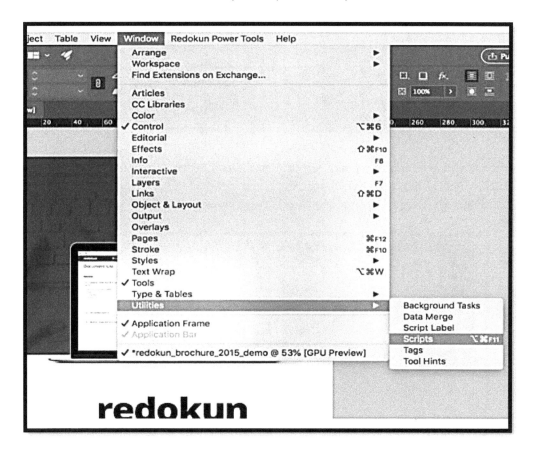

2. Go to the folder **Application** > **Samples** > **JavaScript** in the Scripts Panel.
3. Select the appropriate file and set the location by double-clicking **Exportallstories.jsx**.

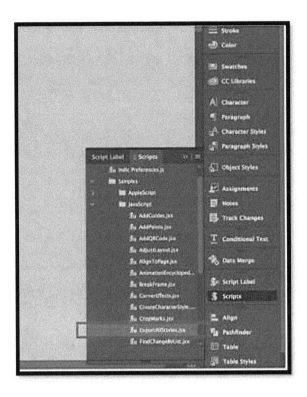

As we already said, the script will make a document for each story in your InDesign file. You should try out all the text formats and then choose the one that works best for you. Since you can export the formatting with RTF, I think your choice will be between Text Only and RTF.

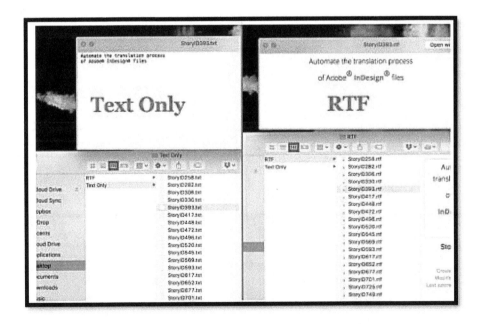

# CHAPTER 5
# USING OBJECT STYLES

Similar to how paragraph and character styles make formatting text easier, Adobe InDesign's object styles make formatting images and frames quick and easy. There are a lot of different choices in these styles, like stroke, color, transparency, drop shadows, paragraph styles, text wrap, and more. An extensive toolset for design customization is provided by the transparency effects that can be applied to the object, fill, line, and text. Object styles can be used on many things, like objects, groups, frames, and even text frames. Styles can change all of an object's settings at once or just some of them while leaving others alone. This is possible by changing the values in the style description, which lets users pick which settings the style affects. If you work with frame grids, object styles make it easy to change how they look.

Any new frame grid starts out with the [Basic Grid] object style, but users can change this style or add more object styles to improve the grid's look. Users can choose factors like writing direction, frame type, and the called grid in the Story Options area when making or changing an object style for a frame grid. Users will notice that many styles have characteristics that are the same, which makes the process of making styles faster. Instead of constantly describing these traits, a new object style can be based on an existing character style. Using this method makes it easier to make new styles because when changes are made to the base style, all shared traits in the "parent" style are instantly updated in the "child" style that goes with it. This layered arrangement of styles helps keep things consistent and speeds up the planning process.

## Defining and applying object styles for consistent design

In just three steps, you can make an InDesign object style. You'll be able to get more done faster because object styles will make your work easier. You know that paragraph styles and character styles work great, right? Actually, object styles work the same way. Book Design Made Simple (see below) has steps on how to set up object styles in InDesign. After creating the object styles in InDesign, using them is the same as using paragraph or character styles. You need to choose a shape, line, text frame, or picture frame that is already set up the way you want it to be before you can make an object style.

**Simply follow these steps:**

1. Click Window, then Styles, then Object Styles to open the Object Styles panel.
2. Choose a shape, line, or frame with the Selection Tool.
3. Select New Object Style from the drop-down menu in the Object Styles window. Type what's shown below into the box, and then click OK.

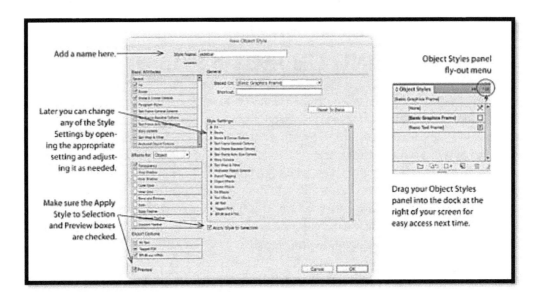

# Updating styles for seamless workflow

It's easy to keep things consistent and make work move more smoothly when you update styles in Adobe InDesign. There are many types of styles in InDesign, such as character styles, object styles, paragraph styles, and more.

**Here is a guide on how to properly change styles:**

1. **Open the Styles Panel:** Start by opening the Styles Panel. To do this, go to the "Window" menu and choose "Styles."
2. **Select the Style to Update:** From the Styles panel, pick out the style type you want to update (paragraph, character, etc.).
3. **Update Paragraph Styles:**
   - If you're changing the style of a paragraph, change the layout of the chosen text to match the new style (font, size, spacing, etc.).
   - To change the style, right-click on it in the Styles panel and pick "Redefine Style."
4. **Update Character Styles:**
   - Choose the text that has the character style you want to update, just like you did with paragraph styles.
   - Make changes to the text's size, color, font, etc.
   - To update the style, right-click on it in the Styles box and pick "Redefine Style."
5. **Update Object Styles:**
   - If you are working with objects, pick out one that has the style you want to update.
   - Make the changes that need to be made, like stroke, fill, effects, and so on.
   - To change the style, right-click on it in the Styles box and pick "Redefine Style."
6. **Based On:** When making or updating styles, use the "Based On" function. By connecting

a new style to an old one, this makes it easier to stay consistent.

7. **Load Styles:** Using the "Load Styles" option in the Styles panel menu, you can import styles from another document or template into your current document.

8. **Update All Instances:** If you update a style, InDesign may ask you if you want to change all cases of that style in the document. Click "Update All" to get a full fix.

9. **Use Object Styles for Consistent Graphic Elements:** Make and use Object Styles for frames, pictures, shapes, and other graphic elements. This keeps the look and style consistent.

10. **Preview Changes:** In the Styles panel, turn on "Preview" to see the changes as they happen in real-time before applying them.

11. **Document-wide Changes:** If you need to make changes that affect many documents at once, use the "Load All Text and Objects" option in the Styles panel menu.

12. **Keep a Style Guide:** To make sure everything is the same, make a style guide for your document. You can put information in this book about fonts, colors, space, and how to use different styles.

Updating styles in InDesign can make your work much easier and make sure that your document looks professional and organized. Reviewing and improving your styles on a regular basis helps keep things consistent and makes it easier to adapt to changes in your design.

# CHAPTER 6
# ADVANCED TEXT LAYOUT

## Text Wrapping and Anchored Objects

### Activating the Text Wrap Panel

**The Text Wrap panel lets you change how each object is wrapped. You can also find the same choices in the menu bar.**

1. The panel will appear when you click on **Window** and then **Text Wrap**.

## Wrap the text

Once you put an object in InDesign, it is set to **No Text Wrap (A).**

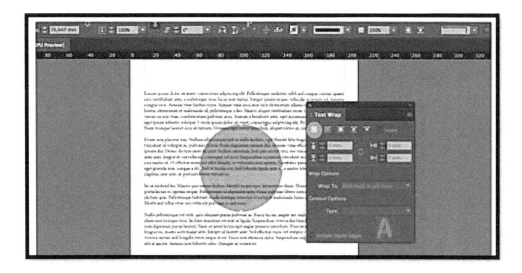

To change this choice, click on the object. You can alter it to:

- **B. Wrap around Bounding Box:** makes the text go all the way around the bounding box.
- **C. Wrap around Object Shape:** This option makes a text-wrap border around the shape you chose. This choice is cool because it can also find the edges of a picture and wrap the text around them.
- **D. Jump Object**: When you use Jump Object, the text will be forced to appear above and below the object. It will not appear next to the object at all.
- **E. Jump To Next Column**: When you click on "Jump To Next Column," the paragraph around it moves to the top of the next column/text frame.

For each choice, this is what happened:

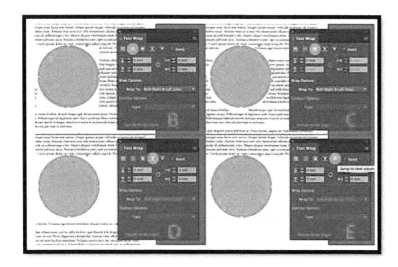

# Adjust the distance between text and object

By changing the offset numbers and the wrap choices, you can change the space between the text and the edges of the object.

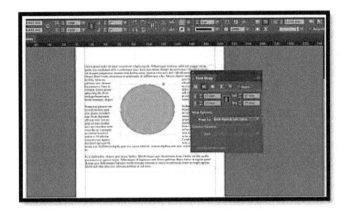

You can later change this boundary by using the Direct Selection tool (the white arrow to be clearer) or the Pen tool.

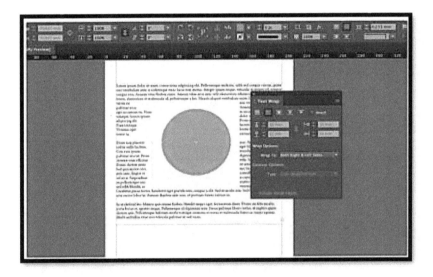

# Detect the edges of an image when text wrapping

When InDesign finds the edge of a picture, it makes a boundary that you can use to wrap text around it (or inside the picture).

1. In the Text Wrap Panel, choose **Wrap around Object Shape**. Next, set the type to **Detect Edges.**

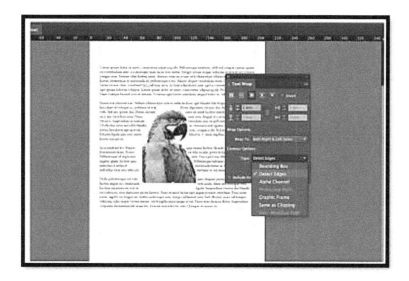

2. You can change how the edges are found by picking the object and going to **Object >
Clipping Path > Options**.

# Wrap text around images with caption

As a whole, a group of objects works like a single object. Putting an image and a description into
a group and then setting Text Wrap to the group is the best way to wrap the text around the
image and caption.

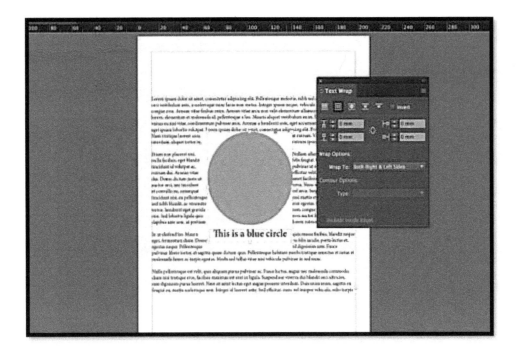

## Wrap text around an anchored object or an inline object

The text wrap character properties of an anchored object only affect the lines of text that come after the anchor marker; the lines of text that come before the anchor marker and the line in which the anchor marker is placed are unaffected by these characteristics. Inline things are also anchored objects, so the same rule applies to them as well.

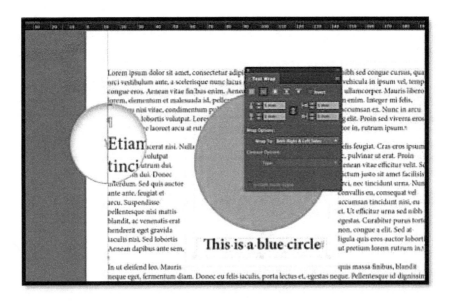

# Text wraps and master pages

You can choose to have the text always wrap around the picture around objects that are put into master pages (this is the usual setting when Text Wrap is turned on), or you can turn on the Apply to Master Page Only option to only apply the text that is put into the master page.

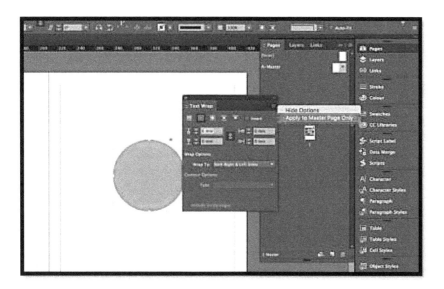

# Text wrap and hidden layers

If you don't hide the layer that a wrap object is connected to, it will still affect text frames in all of them. The choice to **"Suppress Text Wrap When Layer Is Hidden"** will be available in the Layer Options dialog box. When you choose this option, the behavior can be changed. The text that is placed on other levels can be rearranged as a result of this choice.

# Create an anchored object

If an object isn't ready to be put on the page, you can make an empty anchored frame to hold information that you will be able to add later. For example, section text that hasn't been written yet. You can change the size of the connected frame at any time, and the position settings for the frame will change right away.

1. **First, do any of the following:**
   - To add an object that is anchored; first use the Type tool to set an entry point where you want the object's anchor to show up. Then, either drag and drop the object into place or paste it there.

Text can go beyond the downloaded picture, or you may see extra space above the line if the object's frame is longer than the text line it's in. If this is the case, the picture you imported won't show up. You may be able to change the size of the inline object, choose a different anchored object location, add a soft or hard line break, or change the leading value for the lines that surround it.

   - To anchor an object, first choose it and then go to **Edit** > **Cut** from the menu that comes up. The next step is to set the entry point with the Type tool where you want the object to show itself, then select **Edit** > **Paste** from the menu. The location of the attached object is inline in the default setting.
   - If you want to make a placeholder frame for an object that isn't available yet, like text you haven't written for a sidebar, use the Type tool to find the point where you want the object's link to show up. Then, from the menu that comes up, choose **Object** > **Anchored Object** > **Insert**.

Before you can connect text characters, you need to make sketches of the text around them. Each character of text is instantly turned into an inline fixed object when outlines are made.

2. Pick out the object you want to place with a selection tool. Then, from the menu that comes up, choose **Object** > **Anchored Object** > **Options**. You can choose which choices you want.

You might not have to go through the Anchored Object dialog box first if you use the computer function for Insert Anchored Object/Go to Anchor Marker. In the Text and Tables area, you can find the Keyboard Tool Editor. You will need to give shortcut keys to this tool there. If you press the shortcut twice, the object is removed from the selection, and the mouse is returned to the main text.

# Creating and Formatting Tables

Rows and columns are used to arrange the cells that make up a table. You can add text, inline graphics, and other tables to a cell, which works a lot like a text frame with the same name.

Making a table can be done from scratch or by changing text that already appears in a table. You can also add a table inside of another table. The width of the container text frame is filled by the new table that you make after making the first table. A table is put on the same line as the placement point, which is at the beginning of the line. If you put the entry point in the middle of a line, a table will be written on the line that comes after it. Tables work the same way that inline graphics do: they blend in with the text around them. When the point size of the text above the table changes or when content is added or removed, for example, the table will move between linked frames. It is not possible for a table to be on a text-on-path frame, though. When you use InDesign to make a table, you can also put the table inside a text frame that is already there. If you want, you can also tell InDesign to make the text frame that goes around the table you've made.

## Using the Insert Table Option

1. Use the Type tool to create a table inside a text frame that is already there. Then, place the insertion point where you want the table to show up while you are drawing.
2. Go to the menu and choose **Table > Insert Table.**

**The "Create Table" choice can be chosen if the mouse is not in a text frame at the moment.**

3. Say how many rows and columns are in the table as a whole.
4. If the information in your table will go across more than one column or frame, you will need to say the number of header or footer rows you want the information to appear again.

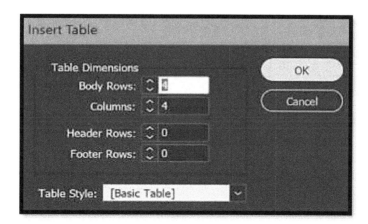

5. Pick a table style (you don't have to do this step).
6. Click the "OK" button. The new table will take up the whole width of the text frame.

## Using the Create Table Option

When you will be using the Create Table option to make a table, it is not necessary to first create a text frame in your document. When you're done drawing the table on the page, InDesign will make a text frame that is the same size as the table right away.

1. Go to the menu and choose **Table > Create Table.**

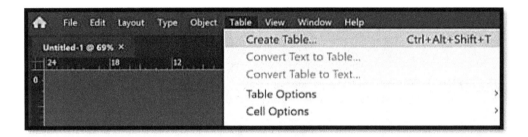

**Additionally, the Insert Table option can be used if the mouse is currently in a text frame.**

2. Say how many rows and columns are in the table as a whole.
3. If the information in your table will go across more than one column or frame, you will need to say the number of header or footer rows you want the information to appear again.

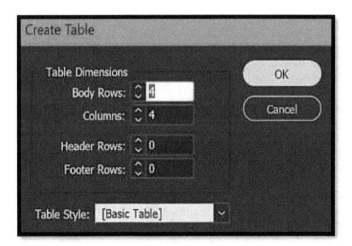

4. Pick the table style you want.
5. Click the "OK" button.
6. You need to use the Table cursor to create the table you want.

The table is put inside the text frame that InDesign makes, which is the same size as the area that was drawn. For each table, the row height will depend on the table style that is chosen. For example, cell styles can be used in a table style to arrange different parts of the table. If any of these cell styles have paragraph styles in them, the leading number of the paragraph styles determines the row height of that area. As long as there are no paragraph styles on the page, the document's default slug sets the row height. The starting number determines the slug. In this case, the slug is the height of the underlined text in the picked text for this talk.

## Create a table from existing text

**It is important to make sure that the text is formatted properly before turning it into a table.**

1. Separate the text into columns by adding tabs, commas, paragraph returns, or any other character. This will get it ready for change. You can use any character, like tabs, commas, paragraph returns, or anything else, to tell rows apart. "There are many times when text can be turned into a table without any changes needing to be made."
2. Figure out the text you want to turn into a table by selecting it with the Type tool.
3. From the menu, choose **Table > Convert Text to Table**.
4. For both the Column Separator and the Row Separator, you need to mark the start of new rows and columns. There are three options for the column and row separators: Tab, Comma, and Paragraph. You can also type a character, like the semicolon (the ;), to use as a divider. Any character you type will show up in the menu with the table the next time you make one from text.
5. You will need to tell the script how many columns you want the table to have if you want to use the same divider between rows and columns.
6. If you want, you can format the table by choosing a table style.

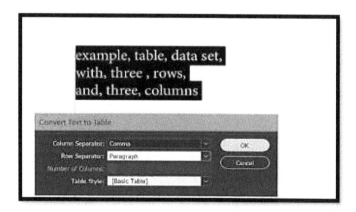

7. Click the "OK" button.

If any rows don't have enough things for the number of columns in the table, the empty cells are filled in.

# Insert/embed a table inside of another table

**What to do:**

1. **First, do any of the following:**
   - Pick out the cells or table you want to embed. Go to **Edit** > **Cut or Copy** from the menu that comes up. Place the entry point in the cell where you want the table to show up. Next, go to the menu bar and select **Edit** > **Paste**.
   - When you click inside a cell, a menu pops up. Choose **Table** > **Insert Table** from that menu. Then, set the number of rows and columns, and finally click OK.
2. Make any changes to the cell inset that are needed.

You will not be able to use the mouse to select any part of the table that goes beyond the edge of the cell if you make it inside a cell. To fix this, you should either make the row or column bigger, or you could put the entry point at the beginning of the table and use the keyboard to move it and pick text for the table.

# Formatting Tables

The Control panel or Character panel can be used to style text inside a table in the same way it can be used for text outside of a table. There are two main window boxes that help you arrange the table: Table Options and Cell Options. With these window boxes, you can change the number of rows and columns, add more table formatting, change the space above and below the table, and change the way the border and fill look. You can use the context menu, the Control panel, or the Table panel to change how the table is set up. By right-clicking (on Windows) or Control-clicking (on Mac OS), you can bring up a context menu with table options after you've selected one or more cells.

## Adjust tables, rows, and columns

You can change the size of columns, rows, and tables in a lot of different ways.

## Resize columns and rows

**How to do it:**

1. Pick out the cells from the columns and rows that you want to change the size of.
2. **Do any of the following things:**
   - In the Table panel, set the Column Width and Row Height settings.
   - Choose **Table** > **Cell Options** > **Rows and Columns**. Then, enter the values you want for Column Width and Row Height. Finally, click OK to finish.

If you choose the "At Least" option for a minimum row height, rows will get taller when you add text or make the points bigger. It doesn't matter if you add or remove text when you choose exactly for a fixed row height. There is often an overset situation in the cell when the row height is fixed.

- The double-arrow icon will show up when you move the pointer over the edge of a row or column. Then, drag the sliders up or down to change the height of the row or left or right to change the width of the column.

Row height is set by the slug height of the current font. So, changing the row height setting or the point size of the font across a row of text also changes the row height. The maximum row height is set by the Maximum option in the Rows and Columns section of the Cell Options dialog box.

## Adjust columns or rows without affecting the table width

**You can change the number of columns or rows without changing the width of the table. To do this:**

- Hold down Shift and drag an inner row or column edge (not the table border). As one row or column gets smaller, the other ones get bigger.
- To make rows or columns fit better, hold down Shift and drag the bottom or right edges of the table.

Hold down Shift and drag the right table edge to change the sizes of all the columns. Hold down Shift and drag the bottom table edge to change the sizes of all the rows.

## Resize the entire table

**The steps:**

1. Use the Type tool to move the pointer to the bottom right corner of the table until it turns into an arrow shape. This will change the size of the table. For the table's height and width to stay the same, hold down Shift.

**Note:** If the table in a story spans more than one frame, you can't use the pointer to make the whole table bigger.

## Distribute columns and rows evenly

1. Pick the cells in rows or columns that are the same width or height.
2. Go to Table and choose either **Distribute Columns Evenly** or **Distribute Rows Evenly**.

## Adjust the distance before and after a table

1. Once the insertion point is in the table, go to **Table** > **Table Options** > **Table Setup**.
2. Different values should be chosen for Space Before and Space After under Table Spacing. Then click OK to finish.

When the space before the table is changed, the space between the rows of a table that ends at the top of a frame stays the same.

# Add text to a table

People can add things like text, anchored objects, XML tags, and other tables to table cells. If you don't set a fixed row height, the height of a table row will grow to fit more lines of text after they have been added. It's not possible to add footnotes to tables.

**These are the steps:**

1. **Choose one of the following options while using the Type tool:**
   - After putting the entry point in a cell, the text should be typed in. Press either the **Enter** or **Return** key to start a new phrase in the same cell. You can move through the cells by pressing the **Tab** key. Pressing Tab in the last cell will start a new row. Click and hold on **Shift** and **Tab** to go back through the cells.
   - To paste the text, first copy it, then move the entry point to a cell and paste it. Then, go to **Edit** > **Paste**.
   - Choose **File** > **Place**, then double-click a text file. Then, put the entry point in the cell where you want to add text. This will let you add text right away.

# Add graphics to a table

**The steps are as follows:**

1. You will need to place the entry point in the cell of the table where you want to add the image.
2. **Choose one of the following options:**
   - To choose one or more image files, from the menu, choose **File** > **Place**.
   - In the CC Libraries panel, pick out a few pictures from the pictures section. Then, drag and drop them where you want them to go. You can also look at the pictures on the placegun.
3. To put the picture or pictures you want to use, just click inside each table cell.
4. **Choose one of the following options:**

InDesign pieces that are in the Graphics section of the CC Libraries panel can't be moved around by dragging and dropping. If you add a picture that is bigger than the cell, the cell's height will grow to fit the picture. The cell's width will stay the same, though, and the image may go past the right edge of the cell. If the row where the graphic is placed is set to a specific height, the cell will be pushed out of line if the graphic is taller than the row height. This happens after the row height is set. If you move the picture outside of the table, change its size, and then copy and paste it into the cell that goes with the table, you can avoid having a cell that is overset. Using the following methods, you also have the option of adding pictures to table cells.

   - You will be asked to set the settings after choosing **Object** > **Anchored Object** > **Insert**.

After the fact, you can add a picture to the connected object.

- To paste a picture or frame, copy it first, then find where you want to put it, and finally choose **Edit** > **Paste** from the menu.

## Add table headers and footers

If you make a long table, it can go past more than one column, frame, or even the whole page. By putting heads or footers in the right places, you can repeat the information at the top or bottom of each different part of the table.

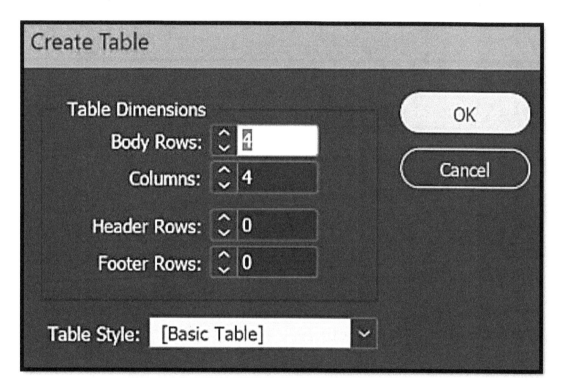

The option to include rows for the header and footer is available when you build the table. You can also add rows for the header and footer and change how they are shown in the table in the Table Options dialog box. You can change the rows in the body to rows in the header or bottom.

## Convert existing rows to header or footer rows

**Here are the steps:**

1. Pick the rows at the top of the table when you want to make header rows. The rows at the bottom of the table are where you can add footer rows.
2. From the drop-down menu, choose **Table** > **Convert Rows** > **To Header or Footer**.

## Change header or footer row options

**What to do:**

1. Put the entry point inside the table and then choose **Table** > **Table Options** > **Headers and Footers** from the menu that comes up.
2. You should say how many rows are in the header or footer. You can add new rows to either the top or bottom of the table.
3. Say whether the information in the header or footer is shown in each text column (if the text frame has more than one), just once per frame, or only once per page.
4. Pick the right option if you don't want the header information to show up in the first row of the table. If you do not want the information about the footer to be shown in the very last row of the table, select the **"Skip Last"** option. When you want to show that the header or footer is longer, the **Skip First option** is very helpful because it lets you do that. Take the example of a table that goes across several pages. To make the opening text say **"Table 2 (Continued),"** select **Skip First** and then place Table 2 in the first row of the table. This is done so that the word "(Continued)" doesn't show up at the start of the table.
5. Click the "OK" button.

# Long Document Features

1. Open Adobe InDesign 2024 for the first time.
2. Access **"File"** > **"New"** > **"Book."**
3. Click on the "+" sign in the Book panel.
4. Find the InDesign files that you want to use in your book and click on them.
5. Click **"Open"** to add them to the book.

6. The Book panel (Window > Book) shows all the files that are part of the book. You can move documents around the screen by dragging them to get the chapters or parts in the right order.

7. To make sure everything is the same, use master pages and modify styles in all of the book's papers. You can set up and change styles and master pages in a single document. To make these changes appear in all of your papers at the same time, right-click and select **"Sync All Documents."**

8. Use the **"Numbering & Section Options"** in the Pages panel to set up automatic page numbering. Put the **"Page Number"** marker on master pages to add page numbers.

9. To divide your book into parts, use the **"Start Section"** option in the Pages panel. For each part, you can add a different table of contents or use this to give each area a different numbering style.

10. A customizable TOC can be made with the **"Table of Contents"** feature. Based on the paragraph styles you choose; InDesign will update the TOC automatically when the content changes.

11. To make it easier to find your way around digital books and PDFs, add favorites. From the **"Hyperlinks"** panel, choose **"New Hyperlink Destination"** to make bookmarks.

12. To make changeable links, use cross-references in the text. If the page numbers change, InDesign will change any links to other parts or chapters immediately.

13. If your book needs an index entry, use the **"Index"** panel to make notes on index items. Pick the **"Generate Index"** option in the Index panel to make the index.

14. Use **"Package"** to get all of the related fonts and pictures in your paper into one zipped file. This is very important for printing or sharing, making sure that all the tools you need are available.

15. Use the right export options for each file (PDF, EPUB, etc.) to make sure the text is ideal for the result you want.

16. To keep track of all the different copies of your book, use dates or version numbers. Share individual files or the book file to work together.

17. Use the Preflight screen to look over the document for mistakes and missing information before you finish it. If you want to print your book, make sure your work meets the standards for print production by inspecting it before it leaves.

# Managing lengthy documents with book features

1. **Create a Book File:**
   - Open Adobe InDesign and make a new book cover document.
   - Choose "File" > "New" > "Book..."
   - Give the book file a name that makes sense.

2. **Add Documents to the Book:**
   - To add documents to the book, go to Window > Book and click on the "+" icon in the Book panel.
   - Pick out all the InDesign documents (chapters) you want to use and click "Open."

3. **Arrange Documents:** Drag the documents around in the Book panel to put them in the

order you want.

4. **Page Numbering:** Make sure that the page numbers are the same in all of your papers. Pick "Numbering and Section Options" from the Book panel menu to set up how pages are numbered.

5. **Sync Styles and Swatches:** Make sure that all of your papers use the same paragraph styles, character styles, and swatches. To get styles and swatches to work together, use the "Sync" button in the Book panel.

6. **Master Pages:**
   - Use master pages to make sure that all of the book's headers, footers, and page sections look the same.
   - Change the master pages in one document, and then use "Sync" to make the changes appear in all of the books' documents.

7. **Table of Contents:** Use the Book panel to make a table of contents. It's time to add the TOC. To do this, go to **"Layout"** > **"Table of Contents"** and pick the book from the **"Style"** choice.

8. **Cross-References:** For changing links in a text, use cross-references. This is very helpful for citing tables, figures, or chapters.

9. **Footnotes and Endnotes:** Make sure that all of the footnotes and endnotes are managed the same way throughout the whole book. You can sync and change footnote and endnote settings in the Book panel.

10. **Indexing:** If your document needs an index, use the Book panel to make one and keep track of it. You can make an index that covers more than one document.

11. **Book Panel Options:** Look at the Book panel menu for more options. For example, "Export Book to PDF" lets you make a single PDF file from all the papers in the book.

12. **Preflight:** Use the Preflight screen often to look over your papers for mistakes or problems.

13. **Package for Printing or Distribution:** When you're ready to print or share the book, use the "File" > "Package" option to get all the linked files, fonts, and other things you need.

14. **Version Control:** Save different copies of your book file so you can keep track of changes and versions. To tell them apart, use version numbers or dates.

15. **Backup Regularly:** To avoid losing data, back up your book file and any other papers that are linked to it often.

# Creating and updating tables of contents and indexes

## Create tables of contents in books

**Before writing the table of contents for a book, make sure to do the following for the best results:**

- Before you make a table of contents, make sure that the book list is complete, that all of the papers are mentioned in the right order, and that all of the headers have the correct paragraph styles.

- Make sure that all of the paragraphs in the book use the same style. Do not make papers with styles that have names that sound like they mean different things. If there is more than one style with the same name but different definitions, InDesign uses either the first instance of the style in the book or the style description found in the current document.
- If the necessary styles aren't available in the Table of Contents dialog box's pop-up options, you'll need to synchronize the book so that they are applied to the document that holds the table of contents.
- No chapter numbers should be used if you want number prefixes like 1-1, 1-3, and so on to show up in your table of contents. Instead, use section numbers. Part names can have a table of contents prefixes added to them.

# CHAPTER 7
# IMAGES AND GRAPHICS

## Insert Pictures and Images

### Inserting Images Using the Place Command

The Place command is the main way that pictures are brought into InDesign. To use the Place **function to add a picture, do these things:**

1. Open your InDesign file and go to the page where you want to add the picture.
2. Click on "Place" in the "File" menu or press "Ctrl+D" (Windows) or "Cmd+D" (Mac) on your computer.
3. Find the place where you saved the picture file and click "Open."
4. The picture will now be in your cursor. You can click and drag to make a frame that fits the picture to the size you want.

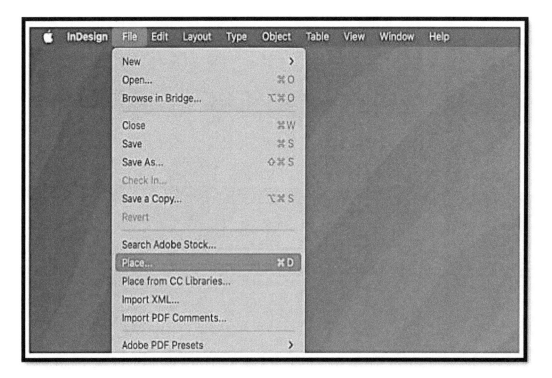

## Working with Images in InDesign

There are a number of tools and methods you can use to control and change your picture once it has been added to your document.

# Resizing and Scaling Images

**Follow these steps to change the size of a picture in InDesign:**

- Use the "Selection Tool" (V) to choose the picture frame.
- To change the size of the frame, click and drag one of its handles. Hold down the "Shift" key while moving to keep the image's aspect ratio.
- In the "Control" or "Properties" panel, check the "Auto-Fit" box to make the picture fit the frame properly.

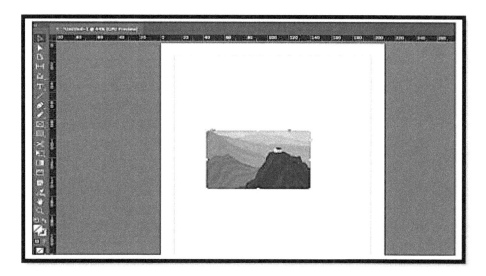

# Adjusting Image Fitting Options

**When it comes to putting pictures into their frames, InDesign gives you a number of options. To get to these options:**

- Use the "Selection Tool" (V) to pick out the picture frame.
- To get to the fitting options, click the "Content Fitting" button in either the "Control" or "Properties" panel.
- Pick a fitting option from the drop-down menu, like "Center Content," "Fit Content Proportionally," or "Fill Frame Proportionally."

# Formatting Image Frames

**You can also change the look of picture frames by adding strokes, changing corner effects, and adding other visual effects:**

- Use the "Selection Tool" (V) to pick out the picture frame.
- To change the stroke width, corner effects, and other formatting options, you can use the "Control" or "Properties" panel.

## Managing Images in the Links Panel

**InDesign's Links panel helps you keep track of all the pictures you've added to a project. To get to the Links panel, press "Window" and then "Links."**

- You can update or relink pictures from this panel if their source files have changed.
- Look at things about the picture, like the file size, color mode, and resolution.
- Use the "Edit Original" function to open the picture in the program that made it so you can make more changes.

# 4 Tips for Working with Images in InDesign

## Tip 1: Use the Frame Fitting Options

When working with pictures in InDesign, it's important to make sure they fit right in their frames. Right-click on the picture frames and chooses "Fitting" to get to the Frame Fitting Options. You can choose from different fitting options, like "Fit Content Proportionally," "Fill Frame proportionally," or "Fit Content to Frame." This makes sure that your pictures keep their aspect ratio and don't look skewed or stretched.

## Tip 2: Maintain Image Resolution

Maintaining the sharpness of your pictures is very important if you want to get good print results. The Links panel in InDesign tells you about the size of the pictures you've put, which helps you keep an eye on their quality. For print projects, you should aim for a resolution of at least 300 PPI. If you need to, you can use the "Relink" option in the Links panel to swap out low-resolution pictures for high-resolution ones.

## Tip 3: Use Clipping Paths for Complex Image Shapes

Cut out the background of a picture with a complicated shape or place it where you want it. This will give your work a clean, professional look. You can use an image editor like Adobe Photoshop to make a clipping path, and then bring the picture into InDesign.mPick out the picture frame, click on the "Object" menu, pick "Clipping Path," and then pick the right path from the dropdown menu. This will make it easier for you to add the picture without any problems to your plan.

## Tip 4: Use Libraries to Organize and Access Images

Using InDesign's Libraries tool, you can easily organize and get to your pictures. You can store and organize your pictures in libraries, which makes it easy to find them and use them in more than one document. You can make a new library by going to "File" and selecting "New > Library." After that, you can drag and drop pictures from your computer or other InDesign files into the library to make it easy to find and use again. This makes your work easier and helps you stay consistent across all of your projects.

# Placing and linking images for dynamic updates

You need to learn how to keep and update image links so that you can easily add graphics to your designs. When you add an image, a version of the file that fits the screen is shown in the plan. This lets you look at the picture and move it around in the plan. **There is a chance, though, that the real image file will be added or linked.**

- The artwork that is connected to the document is linked to it, but it still exists separately from the document. This makes the document smaller. Though transformation tools and effects can be used to make changes to linked artwork, it is not possible to pick out and change specific parts of the artwork. It is possible to use the linked picture in more than one way without making the page much bigger. One more thing that can be done is to change all the links at once. When you export or print, the original image is brought back to life. This means that the end output is made from the originals at their full quality.
- The artwork that is inserted is put into the page at its full size, which makes the paper bigger in the end. Your document is self-sufficient as long as the artwork is inserted; you can keep track of versions and make changes to the file whenever you want.

You can check the Links panel to see if the image is linked or embedded and to change its state from one to the other. Instead of the screen-quality version of a bitmap picture that you put into your layout that is 48K or less, InDesign will immediately use the full-resolution image. These pictures are shown in the Links panel by InDesign so that you can keep track of different versions and make changes to the file whenever you want. But you don't need the link for the best results. These pictures are shown in the Links panel by InDesign. Moving a document to a different folder or disk is important, like when you send it to a service provider. You must also move the picture files that go with the document. These files are not saved with the text. You can instantly copy all linked files when you use the Preflight and Package features.

## Links panel overview

There is a list of all the files that have been added to a document in the Links panel. In this group are both files that are stored directly (on a disk) and assets that are managed on a computer. It is important to know that Internet Explorer does not show copied and pasted files from websites in this panel. The InCopy Links tab also shows items that are linked to each other. Find out about the number of notes, the controlled status, and the status of tracked changes in the Link Info area when you select a linked story in the Links panel. In this place, you can also see the status of tracked changes. If the same picture shows up more than once in the document, the links will be grouped together in the Links box and shown as a triangle with a disclosure triangle inside it. When an EPS or InDesign file that is linked has links, those links are also combined under a transparency triangle. This does happen in some situations. If the situation calls for it, the Links panel can show a related file in either of these ways:

# Up to Date

When the file is up to date, the Status box is blank.

# Modified

The version of the file in your document is older than the version that is saved on the disk if you see this indicator. For example, this signal will show up if you bring a picture you made in Photoshop into InDesign and then change it and save it in Photoshop. The people who do these things could be you or someone else. There is a slightly different form of the changed icon shown when an image is changed and some cases are updated but others are not. This happens when the image is edited.

# Missing

Even though the picture might still be somewhere else, it is no longer at the site from which it was downloaded. Links can be lost if the source file is removed or if it is moved after being imported to a different computer or place. If the source file is not found, it is not possible to tell if a lost file is up to speed. If this icon is present, the file might not print or share at its full size if you try to do some of those things.

# Embedded

While the contents of a linked file are being embedded, management steps for that connection are put on hold. There is an "edit in place" action happening on the given link right now that stops this option from being used. Management tasks will be able to be done on the link again after the file has been removed. If a linked object doesn't show up on a certain page of the document, the symbols PB (pasteboard), PP (parent page), OV (overset text), and HT (hidden text) will show you where the object is.

# Use the Links Panel

- Choose **Window > Links** from the menu bar to open the Links panel. It is possible to tell them apart by the names of all the linked files and automatically inserted files.
- Right-click on a link in the Links panel and choose "Go to Link." This will take you to the linked image. You can click the link's page number in the Page column instead, or you can use the menu in the Links box to choose "Go to Link." The chosen picture takes up most of the space on the InDesign display. You have to show the layer (or condition, if the object is attached) before you can see a hidden object.
- Clicking the triangle icon to the left of the link will let you expand or break linked links. When the same graphic shows up more than once on a page or when the linked EPS graphic or InDesign file has links in it, nested links may appear in the document.
- To sort the links in the Links panel by category, click the category name at the top of the panel. This will arrange the panel's links in a certain order. If you click on the same group

again, you can change the order. In this case, if you click on the Page group, the links will appear in the same order they were first shown, starting with the first page and ending with the last page. If you click Page again, the links will go from the most recent page to the most recent page. Panel Options can be used to make the Links panel have more grids.

# Work with the Links panel columns

You can show more categories in the Links box if you want to tell people more about the images. Dimensions and Creation Date are two examples of these categories. You can pick whether the information is shown in the Links panel as a column or in the Link Info area at the bottom of the Links panel. **This is true for all of them.**

1. From the menu that shows up in the Links panel, choose **Panel Options.**
2. There are options under the Show Column heading that you can use to add columns to the Links panel. The linked file is in Folder 0, which is in turn contained within Folder 0. Folder 1 is also contained within Folder 0, and so on.
3. Pick out the boxes under the heading "Show in Link Info" to show the information in the "Link Info" part at the bottom of the panels for links.
4. Press the OK button.

You will be able to change the order of the columns if you pick a column and then drag it to a new spot. You can change the width of the column by moving the column edges. Click on the name of the group you want to sort the links by to see them in ascending order. Click again to put the things in decreasing order.

## Change the Links panel rows and thumbnails

**What to do:**

1. From the menu that shows up in the Links panel, choose **Panel Options**.
2. There are three Row Size options: Small Rows, Regular Rows, and Large Rows.
3. In the Name column and the Link Info area at the bottom of the Links panel, you can choose whether thumbnails of the images are shown. You can use this option for the Thumbnails tool.
4. Press the OK button.

# Working with Vector Graphics

**Placing Vector Graphics:**
1. **Launch InDesign:** Open or make a new document in Adobe InDesign to start working with vector graphics.
2. **Importing Vector Files:**
   - To place something, go to the File menu and select "Place," or press Ctrl + D on a Windows computer or Cmd + D on a Mac computer.

- Pick out the vector file you want to use and click "Open."

**Scaling and Transforming:**

3. **Scaling Vector Graphics:** To change the size of vector images, use the Selection Tool (V). Hold down the Shift key and drag the corner handles to keep the scale proportional.
4. **Rotating or Skewing:** Hover over a corner with the Selection Tool until the rotation icon shows up. You can now rotate or skew the vector image.

**Making Changes to Vector Graphics:**

5. **Entering Isolation Mode:** Use the Selection Tool to double-click on the added vector image to go into an isolated mode where you can make changes.
6. **Editing Anchor Points:** To select particular anchor points, use the Direct Selection Tool (A). When you're in isolation mode, use the Pen Tool (P) to add, remove, or change lines.

**Working with Layers:**

7. **Layers Panel:**
   - The Layers Panel (Window > Layers) lets you change how your document is organized.
   - Change how vector drawings are shown and stacked since they are on different layers.

**Using Color and Stroke:**

8. **Color Adjustment:** To change the colors of vector drawings, go to Window > Color > Swatches or Window > Color > Color.
9. **Stroke Characteristics:** Use the Stroke Panel (Window > Stroke) to make any changes you need to the stroke properties.
10. **Embedding and Linking**: While working with InDesign, you have the option to embed or connect vector images. Embedding makes the file bigger, but it will still be movable. Linking, on the other hand, keeps a link to the original file.
11. **Exporting with Vector Graphics**:
    - When you want to export your InDesign project, make sure you pick a file that works with vectors, like PDF.
    - You should make sure that the **"Preserve Illustrator Editing Capabilities"** option is set if you need to make more changes in Illustrator.

If you follow these steps, you'll be able to work quickly with vector drawings in Adobe InDesign. You can import and transform them, make fine changes, and organize their levels.

## Editing vector graphics within InDesign

Like Adobe Illustrator, InDesign is not a full-fledged vector graphics editor, but it does let you do some things that you need to do for vector editing.

1. After starting Adobe InDesign, you can make a new project or open an old one.
2. Go to **"File"** > **"Place"** in the **"Place"** menu to choose your vector image file, such as an AI, EPS, or PDF file.

3. You have to click on the page first to move the picture. Use the Selection Tool (V) to move and change its size.

## Basic Editing of Vector Files

1. You should use the Direct Selection Tool (A) to pick out specific anchor points or lines in the vector graphic.
2. You can change the size and rotation of the whole visual document with the Selection Tool. Holding down the Shift key will keep the proportions the same while you scale.
3. You can group multiple objects that you have chosen by using the **"Object"** > **"Group"** menu option. To separate, go to **"Object"** > **"Ungroup."**
4. If you go to **Window** > **Object & Layout** > **Pathfinder**, you can see the Pathfinder screen. This panel lets you do basic things like adding, removing, combining shapes, and more.

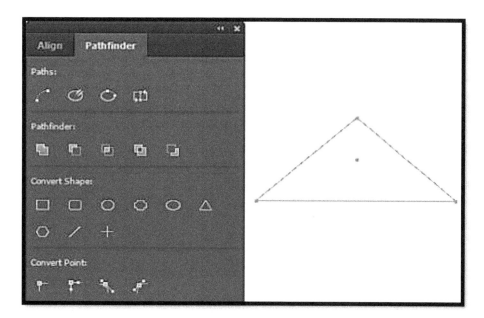

## Stroke and Fill

1. Stroke and Fill options can be found in either the Control panel or the Swatches panel. They can be used to change how the vector image looks.
2. To add stripes and change the clarity, use the Gradient panel and the Effects panel.

## Text and Vector Integration

1. The Type Tool (T) is what you should use to add text to your work. No problems can come up when text and vector images are put together.
2. It's possible to write in creative ways with the Type on a Path Tool because it lets you put text along a vector path.

# Exporting

Go to the **"File"** menu and select **"Export"** to save or send your changes to a PDF, EPS, or any other file type that is easy to access.

## Limitations

- When you compare InDesign's vector work to professional vector tools like Adobe Illustrator, it doesn't have as many features. If you want to make complicated graphic art, you should use Illustrator first and then load the idea into InDesign.
- You can use some live effects in InDesign, but to make more complex effects and filters, you should use Illustrator or Photoshop first and then bring the final design into InDesign.

# Image Manipulation Techniques

1. To choose your picture, go to **"File"** > **"Place"** and click on it. That's not all—you can easily add the picture to your InDesign page by dragging and dropping it.
2. Before moving on, the Place dialog box lets you pick the right options, such as cropping and fitting.
3. To make the picture your choice, click on it. Basic changing options like Cropping, Rotating, and Flipping Horizontally or vertically can only be accessed by going to the **"Object"** menu and selecting **"Image."**
4. Through the **"Effects"** panel, you can change things like brightness, contrast, color, and more.
5. Pick out the picture from the **"Window"** menu, and then pick out **"Effects"** to get to the Effects panel.
6. Find the **"Adjustments"** drop-down menu below the "fx" sign at the bottom of the screen. This will let you change the image's color and tone.
7. You can make different visual effects by changing a picture's clarity or by using different blending modes.
8. To set blending modes or transparency, open the **"Effects"** panel, click on the "fx" button, and pick **"Transparency"** from the choice that appears.
9. You can use either the Pen tool or the shape tools to make a shape over the picture. Make sure both the picture and the form are chosen, then right-click on the picture and pick **"Make Clipping Mask."**
10. You should make picture frames and then move them around if you want to have more control over where photos are placed.

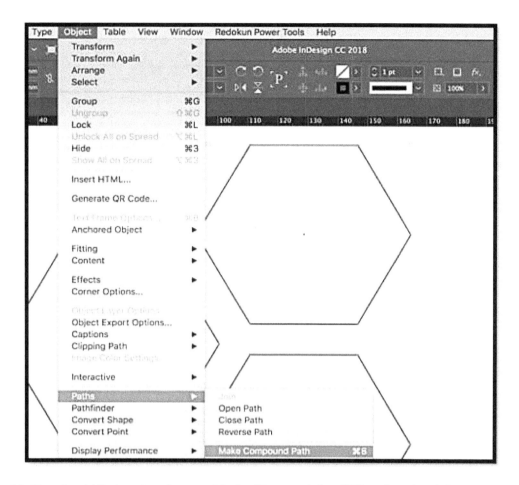

11. You should first make a frame with the **"Rectangle"** or "**Ellipse**" tool and then put a picture inside it.

12. InDesign lets you connect to picture files stored outside of InDesign. If the picture that is linked to is modified, InDesign will add the new version right away.

13. Press "File" and then "Place" to pick out the picture. Make sure the **"Link"** option is chosen in the Place dialog box.

14. InDesign lets you add many different picture effects, such as drop shadow, highlight and emboss and more.

15. Pick out the picture you want to change, then go to "**Window**" > "**Effects**" and pick the "fx" icon from the list that comes up.

16. Make sure that the resolution of your photos is high enough that the quality of the pictures will stay the same when you print them. You can see the image's size by going to "**Window**" > "**Info**" in the menu bar.

17. You have the option to export pictures in a specific file and quality when you export your InDesign document.

# CHAPTER 8
# COLOR MANAGEMENT

## Applying Color to Text and Objects

Color is an important tool for designers, but it can be hard for new users to figure out how to use it in InDesign. InDesign's color options can act erratically at first while you're still getting used to how everything works. This is very annoying and stops you from getting work done. When you're not used to the program, one of the most annoying things can be changing the color of the font. No matter how crazy InDesign seems, there is a method to its madness. Knowing how text color works in InDesign will help you understand and work better with text in InDesign.

## Text Contents vs. Text Frame

It is important to know that InDesign sees the text frame and the text inside the frame as two separate objects when you change the color of the text in it. You can change the background color of both the text frame and the text itself to a different color. This is where most people get lost because if you choose a color for the text frame, it will instead be added to the text itself.

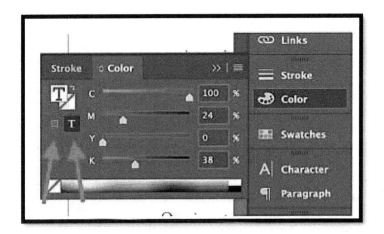

There will always be two options when applying color to a text frame in InDesign: formatting affects the container (shown by the left arrow above), and formatting affects the text (shown by the right arrow above). To change the color of text in InDesign, you need to know the difference between those two things. But there's still one more thing that makes it hard to use. You will have to use the Type tool to pick the text inside the container if your text frame is tied to another text frame. The Formatting affects text option will not work if you choose the frame. You can pick a lot of text from several linked text boxes by placing the text cursor inside the text frame and pressing Command + A (or Ctrl + A on a PC).

# Changing Color Using the Tools Panel

There are color swatches at the bottom of the Tools panel that make it easy to change the color of text in InDesign. To begin, choose the text or text frame that you want to colorize. Keep in mind that if your text frame is linked, you'll need to use the Type tool to pick the text itself instead of just the text frame.

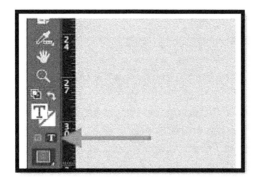

Click the small capital letter T button below the color choices while a text frame is chosen to go to the Formatting affects text mode. If you pick text directly, the Tools box should change to Formatting affects text mode immediately. The color bars will also have a capital T in the middle, as shown below.

If you double-click on the Fill swatch (shown above), the Color Picker dialog box will appear. Click OK after picking the color you want to use. The color of the text you chose will change to match the new one.

## Changing Text Color Using the Color Panel

You can also use the Color panel in InDesign to change the color of text, though you might need to set it up first based on how your workspace is set up. You can show the Color panel if you open the Window menu and choose Color on the list of options. With the Type tool, choose the text you want to colorize. Then, open the Color panel.

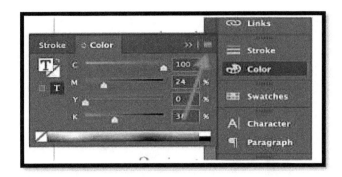

Click the panel menu button (shown above) to open the Color panel menu. Then, choose the color space that works best for your project. Print projects usually use the CMYK colorspace, while screen-based projects use the RGB colorspace. However, you can mix colors in any way you want, since they will all be changed to the correct color space before being exported. If it applies, make sure that the Color panel is set to Formatting affects text. Then, move each slider until you get the color you want. Instead of starting the Color Picker for every small change, this can be a much easier way to make color changes in your plan.

## Using Swatches for Consistent Text Color

If you need to change the color of text across a long document or just want to make sure that all of your text colors are the same, you should become familiar with the Swatches panel. With swatches, you can save colors you use often in a document so you don't have to type them in again every time. This can save you a lot of time.

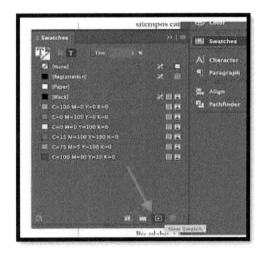

Creating new swatches can be done in a few different ways. You can open the Swatches panel, click the "New Swatch" button at the bottom of the panel, and then double-click your new swatch to make changes to it. Alternatively, you can open the Color Picker dialog window and click the

"Add CMYK Swatch" button. Choose the text or text frame you want to use the swatch on, make sure the Swatches panel is set to Formatting affects text mode, and then click on the swatch you want to use. The new color will be used in your text.

## Change the Color of Multiple Text Boxes

Using paragraph styles and color swatches is the only way to change the color of text in several text boxes that are not linked to each other. Once you've assigned a style to each paragraph, you can change the style in one place, and all the paragraphs that use that style will update to match. Paragraph styles are similar to style templates for text. Basic Paragraph is the name of the basic paragraph style that will be used in all of the text frames you make in InDesign.

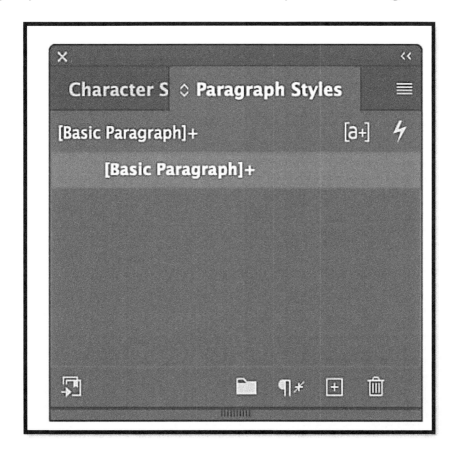

To begin, make a swatch for the color you want to use by following the steps we talked about earlier. Next, open the Paragraph Styles panel. To see the style options, double-click the item that says "Basic Paragraph."

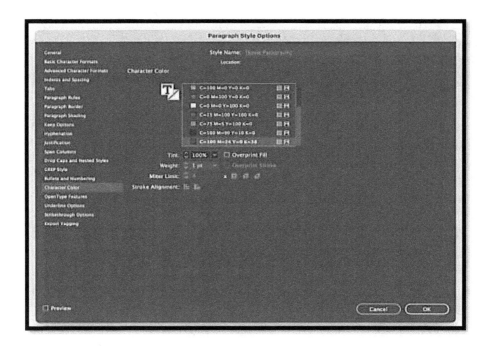

Choose Character Color from the list on the left side of the Paragraph Style Options box. From the list, choose the swatch you made earlier, and then click OK. All of the text that uses the Basic Paragraph style will be changed.

## Why is My InDesign Text Highlighted in Blue?

If your InDesign text is being highlighted in light blue by accident, you won't be able to change it with the color settings in this post because the text isn't colored. When you see light blue text, that's just InDesign telling you that local formatting has been used to override a paragraph style.

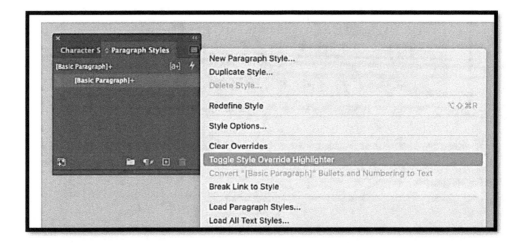

You can turn this off in the Paragraph Styles panel, but it helps to find local formatting in long documents. Toggle Style Override Highlighter is the first item on the menu in the Paragraph Styles box.

# Spot Colors and Color Libraries

- A color-matching method, like the Pantone Matching method (PMS), is often used to choose spot colors.
- A different recipe is used to make each spot color, which makes sure that the colors are the same in all printing methods.

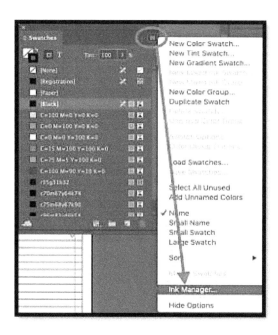

## Creating Your Document

- Open Adobe InDesign 2024 and either make a new document or open an old one.
- Go to "**File**" > "**Document Setup**" to check and change your document's color mode. "**Spot Color**" is great for spot colors.

## Using the Swatches Panel

If you want to see the Swatches panel, go to **"Window"** > **"Color"** > **"Swatches**."

## Adding Spot Colors

To add spot colors, click the **"New Swatch"** button at the bottom of the Swatches screen.

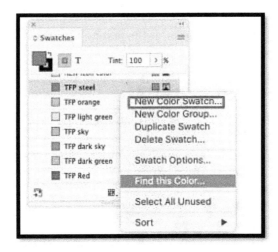

- Choose **"Spot"** as the color type and a selection of spot color libraries, like Pantone.
- Click **"Add"** or **"OK"** to add the spot color you chose to your samples.

## Using Spot Colors on Objects

- Pick out an object or piece of text that you want to apply a spot color.
- Pick out the spot color swatch you need in the Swatches box.

## Checking for Separations

- To make sure your spot colors are applied correctly, go to **"View"** and then **"Overprint Preview."**
- You can see the separations by going to **"Window"** > **"Output"** > **"Separations Preview."**

## Adding Special Effects

- Give the objects with spot colors extra effects like gradients, transparency, or effects.
- Use the "Effects" tab to give the picture glows, drop shadows, and other effects.

## Exporting for Print:

- If you want to export your work, go to **"File"** > **"Export."**
- Check that the file is in a format that can be printed, like PDF, and make sure that **"Include Spot Colors"** is checked in the export options if it's there.

## Using Printers to Communicate

- Make sure your printer can handle spot colors by checking with them.
- Give them a colorproof or swatch book to help them match the colors you want properly.
- Check a copy after printing to make sure the spot colors and special effects are printed the way you want them to be.

# CHAPTER 9
# INTERACTIVE DOCUMENTS

## Creating Hyperlinks and Cross-References

Setting up Text Anchors in your InDesign project and then making a cross-reference to the anchor is a simple process that lets you make documents with a strong and clear related structure. **The process of making a cross-reference to where a text link is located is split into two steps:**

- Make sure the text link is placed where the goal text should be.
- Place the cross-reference at the start of the source text.

**To create the text anchor:**

1. Go to the part of the page that the cross-reference text is pointing to.
2. You can either click to place the text entry point or drag over some text to make it stand out.
3. The Cross-Reference box can be seen from the menu bar by going to **Window** > **Type and Tables** > **Cross-References**.

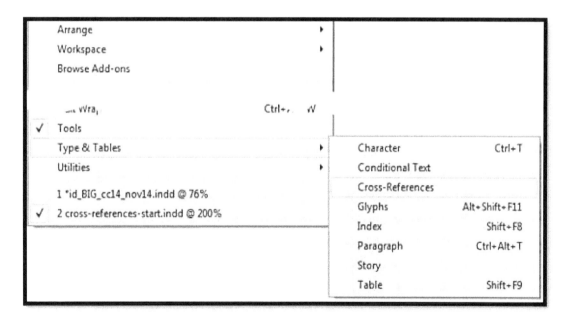

4. In the Cross-References box, choose **New Hyperlink Destination** from the list of options that come up.

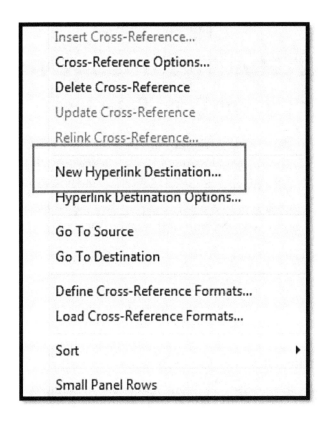

5. A dialogue box for the New Hyperlink Destination appears. For some reason, the Type pop-up option is always set to Text Anchor. If you select some text and then click on the **New Hyperlink Destination command**, that text will stay in the Name field during the whole process. In the Name box, you have the option of giving the text anchor a name. This will make it easy to find if you didn't highlight the text.

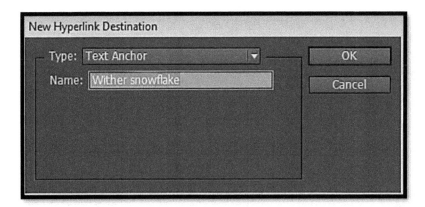

6. If the Show Hidden Characters switch is on, a text anchor sign will appear in front of the text you chose. To move on, click OK.

106

**Follow these steps to make a cross-reference to a text anchor:**

1. Go to the place in the document where you want to add the cross-reference. Next, go to the starting point. An example of the first text that should be used for the cross-reference is "(see)"

2. Second, you need to make sure that the text entry point is exactly where you want the cross-reference text that was made instantly to show up.
3. Find the Cross-Reference panel's menu. Turn on the option to Insert Cross-Reference.
4. In the New Cross-Reference dialog box, choose **Text Anchor** from the list of options that come up for Link To.

5. If the target for the cross-reference is not in the currently open document, use the Document pop-up menu to choose the right one.

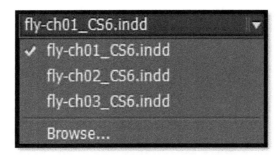

6. Take a text anchor that you've already made and choose it from the Text Anchor pop-up menu.
7. Choose the words that will be in the cross-reference by clicking on one of the options in the window that pops up after you click on Format.

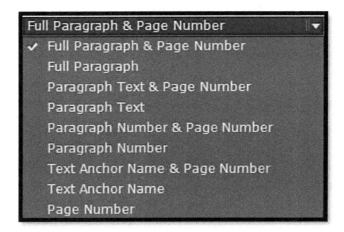

8. When you click the OK button, the cross-reference text and the "page #" markings show up at the Text insertion location. If the "Show Hidden Characters" option is chosen, a cross-reference box will appear around the page number. Also, if the text in your document moves around, the cross-reference page number that is made automatically will be changed to represent the new location of the content that is being cross-referenced.

## Creating Cross-References

1. Make sure you know how the cross-reference text should be formatted before you start making them. Go to **Type > Cross-References** to make new formats for pages, parts, or figures.
2. To enter the cross-reference, move the mouse to the desired spot, then go to **Type > Cross-References,** select the appropriate table style, and then click **"Insert."**
3. To make connections, follow the steps we talked about before, but this time use the cross-

reference marking as the location.

4. You can update cross-references if you make changes to your text by going to **Type > Update Cross-References**. This makes sure that cross-references are correct and show the most up-to-date information.

5. Save your work as a PDF file, and then check the cross-references to make sure they go to the right places.

## Linking content for seamless navigation

1. Click **"Window" > "Interactive" > "Hyperlinks"** to open the Hyperlinks panel.

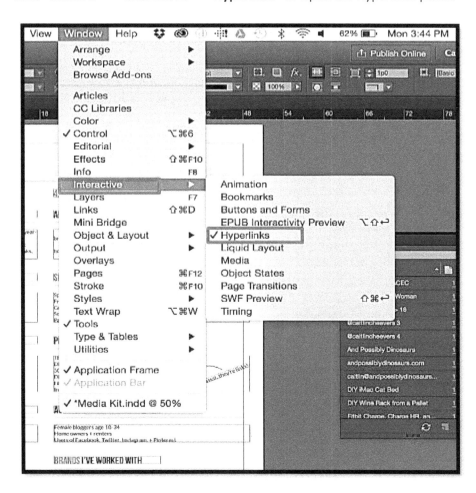

2. Pick out the text or object you want to turn into a hyperlink.
3. In the Hyperlinks panel (the chain icon is at the bottom of the panel), click the **"New Hyperlink"** button. Another option is to right-click on the text or object you want to link to and choose **"New Hyperlink."**

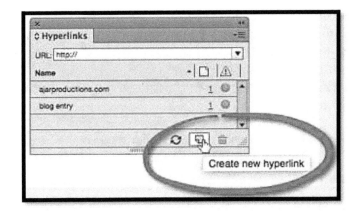

4. **You can connect to a number of places from the Hyperlink Destination text box, such as:**
   - Use the **"Page"** option to link to a specific page in your text.
   - **URL**: A URL is a web address that leads to a website.
   - Use the **"File"** option to link to another file or document.
   - **Text Anchor:** This function lets you link to a specific anchor point on the page.
5. **Once you've chosen the location, you can pick from other options, such as:**
   - **Appearance**: Here you can choose how the hyperlink will look, like making it stand out by underlining it or changing its color.
   - **Highlight:** Use the **"Highlight"** function to choose how the link will look when the mouse is moved over it.
6. You have to go through the steps again if you want to make more hyperlinks.
7. If you want your control buttons to be clickable, make shapes and then turn them into buttons. Simply select the shape, then select **"Window" > "Interactive" > "Buttons"** as the menu option to access the Buttons and Forms panel. Alter the shape so that it looks like a button and set its actions, like "Go to Page."
8. Export your file as a dynamic PDF so you can check the links. Go to **"File" > "Export"** and select Adobe PDF (Interactive) to customize the options. After that, save the changes.
9. The PDF that was made should be opened, and the hyperlinks should be checked by clicking on the text or objects that are linked.
10. The Table of Contents function in InDesign is something you might want to use if your document is broken up into several parts. Since this is the case, you can automatically make links to different parts of your text.

# Cross-referencing within and across documents

## Cross-References within a Document

1. First, load your InDesign file to get into it. Figure out which parts of the information you want to cross-reference, such as the headers, figures, or tables.
2. Moving the mouse to where you want the cross-reference to show up is step two. When

you go to Type, a choice will show up. Choose **Cross-References** from that list. You can choose what kind of reference you want to use in the Cross-References panel. For example, you can choose to use a paragraph, page number, or picture.

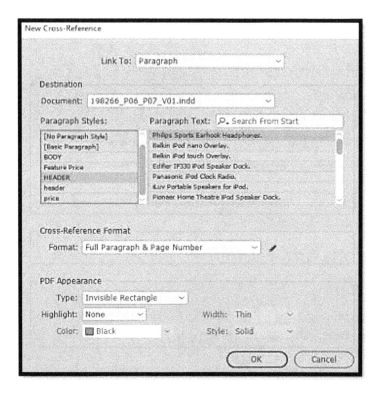

3. Pick out the thing from the list that will be the source, and then click **"Insert."**
4. You can change the way cross-references look by changing the character style that is related to them. Click on **"Character Style"** in the Cross-References window to write your character.
5. If the content changes, you can update the cross-references by selecting them and then clicking the **"Update"** button in the Cross-References box.

## Cross-References across Documents

- Go to **File > New > Book** to make a book file for projects that have a lot of InDesign files.
- By clicking the **"Add Document"** button in the Book panel, you can add your files to the book file.
- To start, go to **Window > Book** and open the Book tab. Double-check that the papers are written in the right way. To make cross-references, paragraph styles, and character styles the same in all of your papers, use the **"Synchronize Options"** option.
- In the Cross-References box, use the **"Book"** dropdown menu to choose the document you want to use as a reference. This is the same process you would use inside a document. To use the paper, you will need to do this.

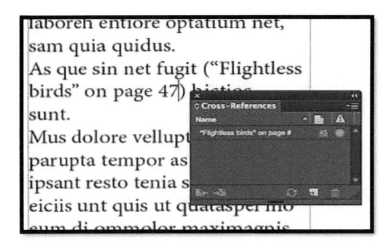

- To change cross-references between all the files in a book, go to the book panel's options menu and choose **"Update References."**

# Adding Buttons and Forms

## Creating Buttons

1. Enter Adobe InDesign and either make a new project or enter an old one.
2. Lay out your paper and style it the way you usually would. Make sure you leave room for things that can be engaged with.
3. To open the Buttons and Forms panel, go to the **"Window"** menu and choose **"Interactive > Buttons and Forms"** from the list. Click on the **"Button"** tool in the panel to choose it.
4. Just click and drag to add a button anywhere on your page. In the Buttons and Forms panel, you can give the button a name, change how it looks, and change how it is laid out.
5. There are three different states that buttons can be in: normal, rollover, and click. The **"States"** panel is where you can change how each state looks. Adding effects like changing the color or the transparency is a good way to make the mood engaging and changing.
6. Go to the Buttons and Forms panel and click on it to get to the **"Actions"** tab. Choose the time the action should happen from the **"Event"** dropdown menu. For example, "On Click." Choose the action you want to take from the **"Action"** dropdown menu. For example, **"Go to Next Page"** or **"Show/Hide Buttons."**

## Creating Forms

- When you're making forms, use the "**Text Field**" tool to make a text field where people can enter text.
- To change how the Buttons and Forms panel looks, you can set a default number and change how the panel looks overall.
- The **"Checkbox"** or **"Radio Button"** tool for drawing should be used to make checks or radio buttons.

- You need to give each checkbox and radio button a name in the Buttons and Forms panel.
- **"Dropdown"** is the tool you should use to make a dropdown list. You can add things to the list that is shown on the screen in the Buttons and Forms panel.
- Put a button on the page and set its action to **"Submit Form"** to make a button that can be used to send that form. The function of a button that clears the form should be set to **"Reset Form."**
- When you use the **"Text"** tool and place the text close to the interactive elements, you can add instructions or tooltips to help users find their way.
- When you're ready to save your work from InDesign, use the **"Preview"** mode to check out the dynamic parts.

# Exploring form field options and functionalities

1. Open Adobe InDesign and make a new project or use one that you already have.
2. To get to the **"Interactive"** panel, open the **"Window"** menu and choose the **"Interactive"** option. In the **"Interactive"** panel, click on **"Forms"** to see the form's choices.
3. Open your file and choose the **"Type Tool"** from the toolbar. Simply click and drag the text frame to place it where you want the form space to show up. When you're done choosing the text frame, go to the "Interactive" panel and find the **"Buttons and Forms"** choice.
4. Decide what kind of form field you want to make. It could be a Text Field, Checkbox, Radio Button, Dropdown List, or Text Field.
5. You can change the features of a text field that you have chosen in the **"Text Field Properties"** window. There are two ways to get to the properties: right-click or double-click on the text field and choose **"Text Field Options."** You can change things like the maximum length of the text, how it looks, and how it is formatted.
6. Set specific settings for radio buttons and checkboxes, such as the export value, the default state, and how they appear. You should double-click on the selection or radio button to get to its settings.
7. You can make a dropdown list by selecting **"Dropdown"** from the **"Buttons and Forms"** menu. You can change the list's features, like the font and appearance, as well as the things that are in it.
8. You can also add activities to form areas to make them more dynamic. Once you've chosen the form field in the **"Buttons and Forms"** panel, click the **"Add New Action"** button during the process. Choose the action that will be taken (like **"Go to Next Page"** or **"Show/Hide Button")** and the event that will set it off (like "On Focus," "On Blur," or "On Mouse Up").
9. To test the form fields, go to **"File"** > **"Export"** and choose **"Adobe PDF (Interactive)."** You should open the exported PDF in a PDF reader that can handle interactive features in order to test your form fields.
10. Don't forget to use the **"Preview"** panel to see how your interactive features work. The "Articles" panel and grouping form areas that are linked to each other can be used to change the order of the interactive elements.

11. Make sure your forms are easy to find by giving the spaces on them the right names or labels. You can change things about form fields, like the alternate text, in the **"Accessibility"** panel.
12. You have to save your InDesign project often to keep the dynamic parts up to date. The live PDFs should be shared with other people so that they can fill them out online.

# Configuring settings for interactive exports

## Method 1: Prepare your Document

- Make sure that the layout of your paper is set up so that it can be interactive. You can add any other interactive elements you want, like buttons, hyperlinks, and video elements that let users interact with the content itself.
- You should use hyperlinks in your text whenever they are needed. They can lead to other pages in the same document, websites that are not in the same document, or email addresses.
- Create interactive buttons in the **"Buttons and Forms"** panel and give them functions like **"Go to Page"** or **"Open URL."** This screen has a button that you can click on to do something.
- Additionally, if your paper has multimedia elements like pictures or music, you need to make sure that they are properly attached or linked.

## Method 2: Access the Export Options

- To save the file in a different format, go to **"File"** > **"Export"** or press Cmd + E (Mac) or Ctrl + E (Windows).
- During the download process, you will need to pick the file you want to use. If you want

your document to have both print and interactive parts, choose **"Adobe PDF (Interactive)"** or **"Adobe PDF (Print)"** for interactive documents.

# Method 3: Configuring the Interactive Export Settings

- Make sure the **"Adobe PDF Preset"** is set to **"High-Quality Print"** or pick a different preset that works for you.
- If you need to, pick the right page range.
- You can change the picture compression settings to fit the needs of your paper.
- Setting the crop marks, bleed, and any other print-related choices should be done whenever it's needed.
- Make sure that the **"Include Hyperlinks"** choice is selected to make sure that the hyperlinks are kept in the saved PDF. Use the **"Include"** menu to choose the right choices for buttons and forms if you have them.
- Customizing any extra advanced choices will help you make them fit your needs.

# Method 4: Export the Document

- Pick a name and a place for the file to be exported.
- If you want to make the interactive PDF, click the **"Export"** button.

# Method 5: Test the Interactive Elements

- Open the produced PDF file in Adobe Acrobat or any other PDF reader that can show interactive elements.
- Please make sure that the hyperlinks work the way they should. Make sure that when you click on the buttons, they do what you want them to do.
- If your project has multimedia parts, you should check that the movies and music work the way you want them to.

**Consider the following further suggestions:**

- If you want to include navigational bookmarks, set them up in your InDesign document before you export it.
- Think about accessibility by adding alternate text to pictures and making sure that people who can help can access the engaging parts.

# CHAPTER 10
# COLLABORATIVE WORK AND VERSION CONTROL

## InCopy Integration

The word processor InCopy is great, and the fact that it works with InDesign makes working together easier. Adobe InCopy lets you change text without changing the way the publication is laid out. This gives the author, editor, or reviewer control over the text and it gives the artist control over how the page looks. Also, they can work on the same document at the same time, like when they're on the same local network. So, whether you are working alone or with a group on an InDesign job, InCopy is a great tool that you should check out.

## Install and set up InCopy

**Are you excited to use Adobe InCopy for the first time? Here are the steps you need to take to get it going on your computer:**

1. Install Adobe Creative Cloud first. You will need to use Adobe Creative Cloud first because Adobe InCopy is part of that suite. For those who don't already have it, you can download it from Adobe's website.
2. Once Adobe Creative Cloud is loaded on your computer, you'll be able to find InCopy in the list of programs you can use. As soon as you click the "**Install**" button next to InCopy, the Creative Cloud app will handle the rest. It might take a few minutes to finish the installation process.
3. Get your work area ready. As soon as you have loaded InCopy, you can change your workspace to fit your needs. Open the "**Window**" tab and pick "**Workspace**." You can choose a current workspace or make your own from this page.
4. You'll need to link InCopy to InDesign if you work with people who use InDesign. From the "**File**" menu, choose "**New**." Then, choose "**Document from InDesign template**." Finally, find the InDesign file you want to work with. You will be able to do the job.

## Collaborative editing with InCopy

1. Share your InDesign file with your team. This is the first thing you need to do to work together. This has to be done to make working together easier. You can do this by putting it as a task in a place that everyone on your team can see.
2. Open the file in InCopy. After that, everyone on the team will be able to open the file. They can choose to open the whole task or just certain parts of it.
3. Once you've opened the file, you can make any changes you want and then save them. It's built into InCopy to remember to save any changes you make to the shared spot while you work. Because of this, the people on your team will be able to see your changes right away.
4. Check out and check in. There is a check-in/check-out feature in InCopy that keeps files from being changed. If you choose to check out an item, no one else can read it until you choose to check it back in. This way, everyone can work on the paper at the same time without getting in the way of each other.

# Managing InCopy assignments and workflows

InDesign is the "**master**" that controls the whole process for both InDesign and InCopy. InDesign is used to make the layout, and it also uses InCopy to prepare materials for the layout and gives jobs and other things. If you could not use InDesign to make a layout and add InCopy content to it, then InCopy would only be a text editor and not be able to make page layouts.

**Here are some of the most important things that InDesign does during the process:**

- Users of InDesign are responsible for using InCopy to add content to a layout.
- People who use InDesign have to put text and picture frames inside a page layout so that people who use InCopy can work without being stopped.
- After the layout is made, the text and picture frames are assigned to it so that InCopy can access its information.

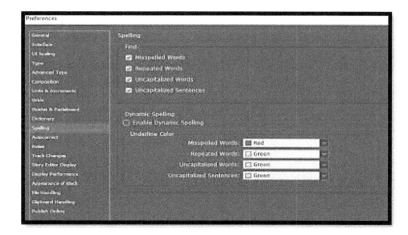

## InCopy's Role in the Workflow

InCopy is a text editor that lets you import and place pictures. It is the part of the process that is in charge of editing. InCopy can use layouts that have already been made, but it can't make layouts itself. It can work with material in layouts, on the other hand. You can also use it to write text (called a "manuscript") that you can then load into InDesign. One of the benefits of writing the text in InCopy instead of Microsoft Word is that nothing is lost when it is sent from InCopy to InDesign. As the editor or author works in InCopy, they can see how the file will be imported into InDesign. In the early stages of the process, you can switch styles to make the copy fit better.

**Here's a rundown of some of the most useful features of InCopy:**

- Text, tables, and other features can be worked with in the same way that InDesign can be used. It is possible to use styles to make the switch from InCopy to InDesign go more smoothly than the usual way, which is to go from Microsoft Word to InDesign.
- InCopy can be used to make new text files. This helps when it comes to putting together the words. InDesign users, on the other hand, are free to add that text to a layout however they want.
- Please note that InCopy can only change text and images that are part of an InDesign layout if the user has directly chosen to do so.
- InCopy can't tell you which parts of a page layout can be changed. The person who uses InDesign makes the choice.
- When you use InCopy on a layout that was made just for it, the software can change the text. You can copy other people's work, but you can't change it.
- It's not possible for InCopy to make a text/picture frame for newly made files. The only things that InDesign can handle are things that are already in frames that it made.
- InCopy can add pictures to picture frames that are already there if an InDesign user has given it permission to do so.

# Versioning and Collaboration Best Practices

Versioning and collaboration are important parts of using Adobe InDesign, especially when working on design projects with other people and adding to a single document. **Here are a lot of the best ways to work together and keep track of versions in Adobe InDesign:**

1. **File Organization:**
   - Make sure your InDesign project's folders are clear and well-organized. Put source files, pictures, and other items in their own folders.
   - Make sure that the names of your files and folders are uniform and detailed so that they are easy to find.
2. **Save As an Incremental Naming:**
   - Use "Save As" often to make copies of your InDesign file that are bigger than the last one. This lets you keep track of changes and quickly go back to an earlier version if

you need to.

- Put a version number or date in the title so that you can quickly see what state the document is in.

3. **Master Pages for Consistency:** Use master pages to make sure that your whole work is consistent. This makes sure that changes made to a master page are made to the whole text, so there are fewer chances of mistakes.

4. **Collaborative Workflows:**
   - When working on a project with other people, make sure everyone knows their clear jobs and duties. Make it clear who is in charge of which parts or pieces of the design.
   - You might want to use Adobe's InCopy for collaborative text editing, which lets artists and copywriters work on the same page at the same time.

5. **Linked Assets:** Instead of adding pictures and graphics, link them to other files. This keeps the size of the InDesign file doable and lets team members change images that are tied to the main page without changing it.

6. **Package and Share:**
   - Use InDesign's "Package" tool on a regular basis to put all of your linked files, fonts, and the InDesign document itself in one place. This makes it easy to share with clients or coworkers.
   - Use a version-controlled tool to share the packed folder so that everyone is working with the same files.

7. **Version Control Systems:** If you work with a lot of people, you should use version control systems like Git or SVN as part of your process. This lets you keep track of changes, handle issues, and go back to earlier versions if you need to.

8. **Communication Channels:**
   - Make sure your team has clear ways to talk to each other. Keep each other up to date on progress, changes, and problems on a regular basis to keep the process running smoothly.
   - To keep conversations and file sharing in one place, use project management tools or contact platforms.

9. **Make regular backups:** Set up a strong backup plan. Back up your InDesign project often so that you don't lose any data if something goes wrong or the system crashes.

10. **Documentation**: Keep detailed records of the project's structure, design choices, and any special directions for team members. This helps new people on the team understand the job right away.

# CHAPTER 11
# PREPRESS AND PRINTING

## Preflighting and Document Verification

A big part of the InDesign editing process is preflight, which is used to fix technical problems like lost pictures or fonts or text that is too close to the edge of the page. There is an open InDesign file here. At first glance, everything seems to be fine. In the bottom left area of the screen, though, there is a small red circle next to some writing that says "3 errors." There are problems with the paper that need to be fixed before you send it to print if there is a red circle here.

If you double-click on the red circle, you can get to the Preflight panel. You can also get to the Preflight panel from the main menu by going to **Window** > **Output** > **Preflight**. First, there is a check box in the upper left corner of the screen that lets you turn Preflight On or off. Preflight should always be on, just in case. This means that As you work, InDesign will actively point out technical mistakes and change them to "**No errors**" as you fix them.

In the middle of the screen is the Error window. This page is where Preflight shows and sorts the mistakes it has found. There is a missing link, as shown in the error message that grows when you click the gray line to the left of the text. If you click the gray line again, you'll see the name of the missing link. It will take you right to the link in your project if you double-click on its name.

Click to choose the link's name in the Preflight panel. Then, click to open the Info window at the bottom of the panel. InDesign is trying to help you by telling you exactly what's wrong and how to fix it. To find the lost file, go to the Links panel and click the **"Relink"** button. The Relink button, which looks like a chain link, is at the bottom of the top part of the Links panel. If the link is missing, it will be marked with a red question mark.

This is where you can find the broken link and click Open to fix it. Now the missing link is fixed, and you can see in the Preflight panel that the error message is gone. I only have two more problems to solve.

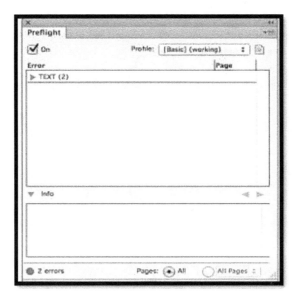

The last few mistakes have to do with text. To find out more about them, click the gray arrows again to see the exact problem and then the exact location of the text error. Overset text means that text is spilling over the edge of a text frame twice here.

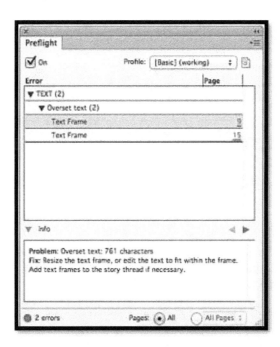

# Print-ready PDF Export

1. **File>Export>Adobe PDF (Print)**

This opens the settings dialogue box for exporting to Adobe PDF

2. **Select 'Adobe PDF Preset: [PDF/X-1a:2001]'**

This setup takes care of most of the settings for you. All RGB colors are changed to CMYK, including photos and all transparency is smoothed so that professional printers and RIPs won't have any problems with it.

3. **Marks and Bleeds** (see picture below)

Check the box next to "**crop marks**," and then type 3mm for the top, bottom, left, and right bleeds.

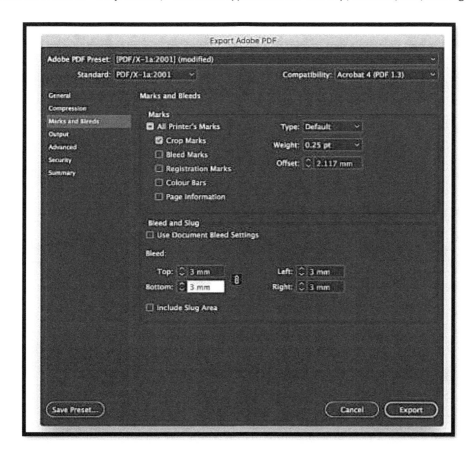

4. **Output>Destination:Document CMYK – Coated FOGRA39 (ISO 12647-2:2004)** (see picture below)

This is where you pick which color profile to use when you change from RGB to CMYK. We have found that the polished FOGRA39 shape gives the best CMYK color change after a lot of tests.

5. **Export**

**Note:** Don't click on "spreads." This makes spreads for readers, not spreads for printers. We need to cut reader spreads back into single pages so that we can put them in.

# Understanding PDF/X standards for printing

There are PDF presets in InDesign that can help you make fewer choices and remember less. Many screens of options are organized by presets into the most common process groups, like business printing, desktop printing, and digital publishing. But can you really trust a setup to take care of the thing you spent so much time making? Also, how are you going to remember all of the different ways to print a PDF every time you need one? Do not worry about the learning curve; InDesign's PDF presets do not work on their own. If you've made PDFs with other Adobe Creative Cloud apps, you'll know some of the basic settings in InDesign. When using Illustrator or Photoshop to make PDFs, the presets are found in similar places. A flyout in the File menu makes it easy to get to InDesign's PDF settings. To see all of your choices, go to **File** > **Adobe PDF Presets**.

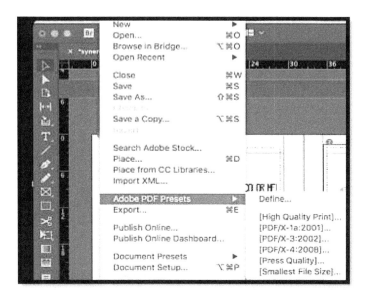

To quickly remember what a certain preset does, go to your InDesign project and choose **File > Adobe PDF Presets > Define.** As you choose a preset, you'll see a simple **"Preset Description"** right there in the dialog box.

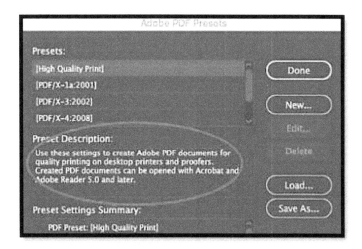

## "High Quality Print" PDF Preset

For this setting, InDesign says that PDF files will be made that can be used for "high-quality printing on desktop printers and proofers." Which settings work best for this app? Photos in color or grayscale that have a quality of more than 300 ppi will be shrunk down to 300. Since the colors aren't changed, RGB and CMYK pictures will stay in the color spaces they were made in. Every setting for openness will also be left alone. Keep in mind that Acrobat and Acrobat Reader 5 are the bare minimum to work with these settings, which shouldn't be a problem these days.

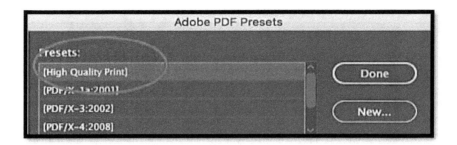

# What is PDF/X?

If your printer hasn't given you any instructions, PDF/X guidelines are the best thing to use. They're a good choice if you want to make sure your printer can open the file and cut down on printing issues. After talking to other makers and leaders in the industry, Adobe put together this set of ISO guidelines for print processes. Printers will often tell people to use the PDF/X presets because these standards are meant to make PDFs that can be printed by more people.

## "PDF/X-1a:2001" PDF Preset

PDF/X-1a:2001 takes away the ability to work with Acrobat 5 and instead uses Acrobat 4. It doesn't matter if your colors are RGB or CMYK; they will all be changed to CMYK immediately. Any spot colors you've chosen will stay the same, though. You will also need to be careful about transparency flattening, and you might want to set the limits for your transparency treatment. Click "**New**" after selecting "**PDF/X-1a:2001**" under **Define** from the list of **Adobe PDF Presets** under **"File."**

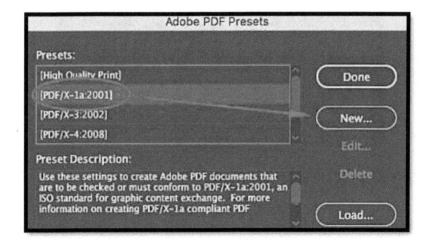

Click **"Advanced"** on the left menu and then click **"Transparency Flattener"** on the right. Pick the **"High-Resolution Transparency Flattener"** setting if you want to keep the quality of your text and files. Photos with resolutions higher than 300 ppi will be lowered to 300 ppi.

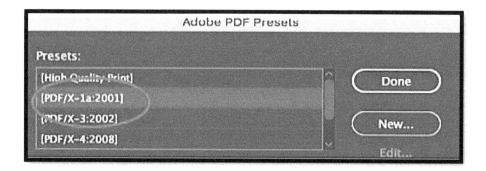

## PDF Preset "PDF/X-3:2002"

This setting will make your transparency flatten. Follow the same steps above if you want to choose your transparency settings ahead of time. PDF/X3:2002 is like the old PDF/X choice in that embedded RGB profiles can be kept (they don't change automatically to CMYK). It's a useful setting if your printer wants to change the color settings based on where you're printing. This format is more popular with printers in Europe than in the United States.

## PDF Preset "PDF/X-4:2008"

You can keep any transparency in your document with this PDF/X present because the support is set to the most recent Acrobat 7. This is the most important thing that the PDF/X-4:2008 file does well. You can also keep any high-resolution photos in good shape. You can use colors like RGB, CMYK, and grayscale. You can still use LAB or ICC settings, and spot colors will not change.

## PDF Preset "Press Quality"

This is another set of choices that are often used with professional printers that print at high quality. You can keep the document's transparency with this setting; you don't have to smooth it first. If you export a file in this way, Adobe Acrobat will be happy with it because it works well with live transparency and makes nice separations. Up to Adobe Acrobat 5 will be able to use it. If the real resolution is higher, all RGB values will be changed to CMYK, and the picture quality will be lowered to 300 pp.

## PDF Preset "Smallest File Size":

**"Smallest File Size"** is used most often on the web, where file size is important. This setting should be used for anything you want to share or show on a screen so that as many people as possible can see your document. Anything that has color and a high resolution will be instantly shrunk to 100 ppi. With up to 150 ppi, grayscale pictures can look very clear. You'll be able to work with files from as far back as Acrobat 6, and your layers and transparency will stay safe.

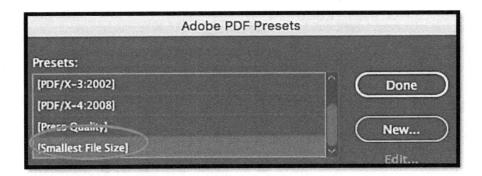

## Custom InDesign Presets

If you work in a business setting with a normal print process, the above choices will almost always get your documents ready to print. InDesign lets you change presets in a number of ways, in case you need to or just feel like getting fancy.

**You don't have to talk about every possible standard change, but here are some ideas for everyday needs:**

- To make your InDesign files dynamic after you've saved them as PDFs, go to File > Adobe PDF Presets > Define. Then, pick the setting you want to use and press "New."

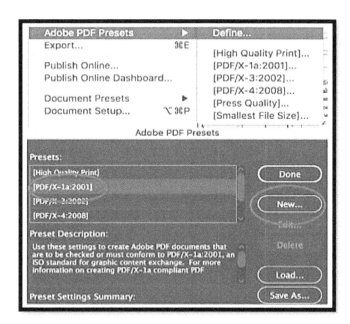

- Choose "General" from the menu on the left, then choose the Hyperlinks and Interactive Elements you want from the list at the bottom of the screen:

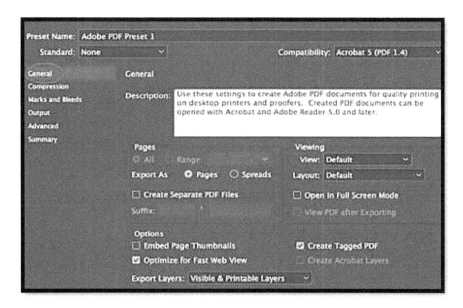

- To add crop marks, bleed marks, or other printer marks that your printer wants, go to File > Adobe PDF Presets > Define, pick your setting, and then press "New."

In the text box, choose "All Printer's Marks" in the upper screen and "Marks and Bleeds" from the choice on the left.

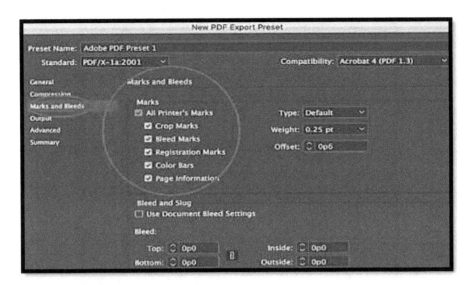

## Saving your PDF Preset

Once you've made any more changes to any of InDesign's PDF Presets, give your preset a name in the box at the top of the screen. Click the "OK" button in the bottom right corner of the box.

Your setting will be put into the Adobe PDF Presets text box without you having to do anything.

# PDF/X Standards Overview

## PDF/X-1a:2001 and PDF/X-3:2002

- **Intended Use:** The main reason for using it is for offset printing with CMYK color.
- **Color Spaces:** You can only use CMYK for color spaces.
- **Transparency:** Live transparency is not supported. All of the openness needs to be smoothed.

- **Fonts:** Fonts need to be built in.
- **Layers:** You can't use layers.
- **Image Compression:** You can't use JPEG 2000 to compress images.

# PDF/X-4:2010 and PDF/X-5g: 2010

- **Intended Use:** The goal is to make it more adaptable and work with more color areas.
- **Color Spaces:** It works with spot colors, RGB, and CMYK.
- **Transparency:** You can be transparent in real-time.
- **Fonts:** Fonts need to be built in.
- **Layers:** You can use layers.
- **Image Compression:** You can compress images with JPEG 2000.

**To make PDF/X-Compatible files, do these things:**

- Get your InDesign file ready.
- Make sure that your document's color mode fits the PDF/X standard. For PDF/X-1a or PDF/X-3, the mode should be CMYK. For PDF/X-4 or PDF/X-5g, the mode should be RGB or CMYK.
- You can give your document the right color profiles by going to "Edit > Assign Profiles" in the menu bar.
- Make sure that every picture and color is in the right color area.
- Use the "**Flattener Preview**" panel for PDF/X-1a or PDF/X-3 to flatten transparency.
- Live transparency is allowed for PDF/X-4 or PDF/X-5g, but keep in mind that there may be problems when you print them.
- From the "**File > Adobe PDF Presets**" menu, choose the right PDF/X setting. Make sure that "Embed All Fonts" is checked in the export settings.
- Change the settings for picture compression based on the PDF/X standard you picked. PDF/X-4 and PDF/X-5g can work with JPEG 2000, but PDF/X-1a and PDF/X-3 can't.
- Figure out what kind of result you want for your paper. This is very important for making sure that colors look the same on all screens.
- Choose Adobe PDF (Print) from the "File > Export" menu. In the Export Adobe PDF window, choose the right PDF/X setting.
- Use the Preflight tool in Adobe Acrobat to look for problems and make sure the file meets the chosen PDF/X standard.

# CHAPTER 12
# AUTOMATION AND SCRIPTING

## Introduction to Scripts

People all over the world who work as workers use Adobe InDesign, which is desktop editing software. Scripts in InDesign are short pieces of code that are used to handle tasks that are done over and over again in the program. These scripts, which are written in JavaScript and can be run inside InDesign, can be used to handle a wide range of tasks and processes. Automation scripts can do tasks that would normally be hard to do and take a lot of time. This can greatly increase productivity and make processes easier.

One of the best things about using automation scripts in InDesign is that they can be used to handle tasks that are done over and over again. In this case, if you often make layouts with a certain style, color scheme, and font, you could make a script that will apply these settings to a new page immediately. This means you don't have to manually set up each piece, which saves you time and effort, keeps things consistent between projects, and lowers the chance of mistakes caused by people. To test, using automatic tools can also be very helpful in many ways. It is very important to make sure that everything is where it should be and working the way it should when you are working on long papers or complicated plans. Tests that look for problems or errors, like lost pictures, broken links, or wrong text layout, can be made with automation scripts. You can also look for types that are missing or make sure that engaging parts work. This way, creators can find issues and fix them before the project is finished. It is possible to simplify the testing process, which lets you find problems earlier and avoid costly mistakes at the same time. Automation scripts can do a lot more than just planning and testing. They can merge data, handle multiple files at once, and send files in different forms, among other things. For instance, if you need to make several copies of a document that are all translated into different languages, you can use an automatic script to put the translated text into the right layouts. This will make the whole process go more quickly and require fewer people to work on it.

# Benefits and applications of automation

## Benefits

1. **Time Efficiency:**
   - **Batch Processing:** Doing things over and over again, like editing pictures, making sure that the entire layout is the same, or changing text in multiple documents, automatically can save a lot of time.
2. **Consistency:**
   - **Uniform Design:** Automation makes sure that styles, formatting, and design elements are used the same way throughout a document or across multiple documents, so the look and feel of all of them stay the same.
3. **Error Reduction:**
   - **Elimination of Manual Errors:** Automating normal jobs lowers the chance of mistakes made by people, which results in more accurate and error-free designs.
4. **Scalability:**
   - **Handling Large Projects:** Automation is especially helpful for taking on big, complicated projects because it streamlines processes and cuts down on the time needed for doing the same things over and over again.
5. **Improved Collaboration:**
   - **Standardization of Workflows:** Automation helps standardize workflows, which makes it easier for multiple team members to work together without any problems and follow the same steps.
6. **Quick Updates:**
   - **Dynamic Content Updates:** Automation makes it easy to quickly change things like prices, times, or contact information that change on multiple pages or documents.
7. **Resource Optimization:**
   - **Reduction in Workload:** Automation frees up designers' time by taking care of boring chores, so they can work on more creative and strategic parts of their jobs.

## Applications

1. **Data Merging:**
   - **Mail Merge:** If you want to make custom papers like letters or brochures by pulling information from a database, you can use data merging features.
2. **Templates and Master Pages:**
   - **Standardized Layouts:** Make templates and master pages to automatically plan parts

that are used over and over again. This way, the structure of multiple pages or papers will be the same.

3. **Object Styles:**
   - **Consistent Formatting:** Object styles make it easy to apply uniform formatting to things like text frames, pictures, and shapes.
4. **Scripts:**
   - **Custom Automation:** You can write your own scripts or use existing ones to handle jobs that aren't covered by InDesign's built-in features. This makes InDesign more useful.
5. **Table of Contents and Indexing:**
   - **Automated Indexing:** Make live tables of contents and indexes based on the content of a document; these will update themselves automatically as the content changes.
6. **Preflighting:**
   - **Error Checking:** Set up preflight settings to check documents for problems automatically before they are printed or exported. This makes sure that the files are ready to print.
7. **Interactive Documents:**
   - **Buttons and Hyperlinks:** for digital or interactive documents, make it easy to add interactive elements like buttons, hyperlinks, and navigating tools by automating the process.
8. **PDF Export setups:**
   - **Streamlined Export:** Make export setups to automatically export documents to different forms with set parameters, making sure that the result is always the same.

# Writing and executing custom scripts

## Accessing the Script Editor

- To get to the Script Editor, start Adobe InDesign on your machine. In your browser, go to **Window > Utilities > Scripts** to get to the Scripts panel.
- In the Scripts panel, you can make new scripts, run existing scripts, and stack them in files if you want to.
- Right-click on the folder in the Scripts panel where you want to make a new script. This will begin the process of making the script. Click on "New Script" and then give it a name.
- Double-click on the script to open it in the script editor.
- This is where you write your JavaScript code.
- Save your script. Pick the story from the Scripts row. At the bottom of the screen, press the Run Script button which looks like a triangle.
- Use console.log () to print information for analysis. Know that the script editor can find issues with grammar.

## Executing Custom Scripts

- To run custom scripts, go to Window > Utilities > Scripts and open the Scripts panel. Go to your script and double-click it to run it.

- Make a new InDesign file or open an old one. Under Edit, click on Keyboard Shortcuts.
- Pick Scripts from the Product Area menu. Make a link for your script.
- When you go to File > Automate > Batch, you can run a script on many files at once.
- Scripts may start running when you do certain things, like open or save a document. You can use the app.eventListeners.add() function to link scripts to events.

# Integrating scripts into the workflow for efficiency

Adding scripts to your Adobe InDesign process may make it much more efficient by handling tasks that you do over and over, improving workflow, and making you more productive overall. The programming languages that Adobe InDesign can read are JavaScript, AppleScript (for macOS), and VBScript (for Windows). Adobe InDesign scripts are written in the computer language JavaScript. Some of the things that scripts can do automatically are making and handling items, saving papers, and editing text.

## Accessing Scripts Panel

- To get to the Scripts Panel, open Adobe InDesign and choose the "Window" option. Go to **"Utilities"** and pick **"Scripts."**

- Adobe InDesign mostly works with JavaScript as a programming language. For macOS users, AppleScript is another option, and for Windows users, VBScript is an option.
- Go to Adobe's website and read through the coding instructions for Adobe InDesign. To learn more about programming objects, properties, and methods, read this material.
- Open a script editor. For JavaScript, use the ExtendScript Toolkit. You can type or copy and paste your script code into the window. When you save the script, use the.jsx ending.
- In the Scripts panel, find the place where your script is saved. Double-click on the script to run it. Scripts can also be linked to special keys or buttons to make them easier to get to.

# CHAPTER 13
# TIPS AND TRICKS FOR EFFICIENCY

## Keyboard Shortcuts

| Tools SHORTCUTS | 🍎 | ⊞ |
|---|---|---|
| Selection tool | V, Esc | V, Esc |
| Direct Selection tool | A | A |
| Toggle Selection and Direct | Cmd+Tab | Ctrl+Tab |
| Page tool | Shift+P | Shift+P |
| Gap tool | U | U |
| Pen tool | P | P |
| Add Anchor Point tool | = | = |
| Delete Anchor Point tool | - | - |
| Convert Direction Point tool | Shift+C | Shift+C |
| Type tool | T | T |
| Type On A Path tool | Shift+T | Shift+T |
| Pencil tool (Note tool) | N | N |
| Line tool | \ | \ |
| Rectangle Frame tool | F | F |
| Rectangle tool | M | M |
| Ellipse tool | L | L |
| Rotate tool | R | R |
| Scale tool | S | S |
| Shear tool | O | O |
| Free Transform tool | E | E |
| Eyedropper tool | I | I |
| Measure tool | K | K |
| Gradient tool | G | G |
| Scissors tool | C | C |
| Hand tool | H | H |
| Temporarily selects Hand tool | Spacebar (Layout mode), Opt (Text mode), or Opt+Spacebar (both) | Spacebar (Layout mode), Alt (Text mode), or Alt+Spacebar (both) |
| Zoom tool | Z | Z |
| Temp selects Zoom Intool | Cmd+Spacebar | Ctrl+Spacebar |
| Toggle Fill and Stroke | X | X |
| Swap Fill and Stroke | Shift+X | Shift+X |
| Toggle between Formatting Affects Container & Formatting Affects Text | J | J |
| Apply Color | , [comma] | , [comma] |
| Apply Gradient | . [period] | . [period] |
| Apply No Color | / | / |
| Switch between Normal View and Preview Mode | W | W |
| Frame Grid tool (horizontal) | Y | Y |
| Frame Grid tool (vertical) | Q | Q |
| Gradient Feather tool | Shift+G | Shift+G |

| Layers Panel SHORTCUTS | 🍎 | ⊞ |
|---|---|---|
| Select all objects on layer | Option-click layer | Alt-click layer |
| Copy selection to new layer | Opt-drag small square to new layer | Alt-drag small square to new layer |
| Add new layer below selected layer | Command-click Create New Layer | Ctrl-click Create New Layer |
| Add new layer to the top of the layer list | Shift+Command-click Create New Layer | Shift+Ctrl-click Create New Layer |
| Add new layer to the top of the layer list and open New Layer dialog box | Cmd+Option+Shift-click Create New Layer | Shift+Alt+Ctrl-click Create New Layer |
| Add new layer and open New Layer dialog box | Option-click Create New Layer | Alt-click Create New Layer |

| Pages Panel SHORTCUTS | 🍎 | ⊞ |
|---|---|---|
| Apply master to selected page | Opt-click master | Alt-click master |
| Base another master page on selected master | Opt-click the master you want to base the selected master on | Alt-click the master you want to base the selected master on |
| Create master page | Cmd-click Create New Page button | Ctrl-click Create New Page button |
| Display Insert Pages dialog box | Opt-click New Page button | Alt-click New Page button |
| Add new page after last page | Shift+Cmd+P | Shift+Ctrl+P |

| Character and Paragraph Styles SHORTCUTS | 🍎 | ⊞ |
|---|---|---|
| Make character style definition match text | Select text and press Shift+Opt+Cmd+C | Select text and press Shift+Alt+Ctrl+C |
| Make paragraph style definition match text | Select text and press Shift+Opt+Cmd+R | Select text and press Shift+Alt+Ctrl+R |
| Change options without applying style | Shift+Opt+Cmd-double-click style | Shift+Alt+Ctrl-double-click style |
| Remove style and local formatting | Opt-click paragraph style name | Alt-click paragraph style name |
| Clear overrides from para-style | Opt+Shift-click parag style name | Alt+Shift-click paragraph style name |
| Show/hide Paragraph and Character Styles panels | Cmd+F11,Cmd+Shift+F11 | F11, Shift+F11 |

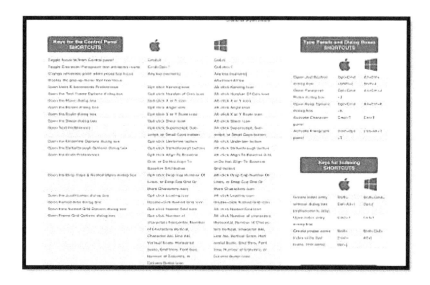

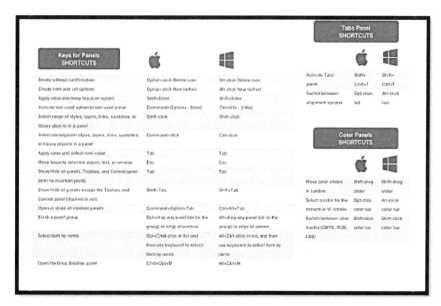

# Creating and customizing shortcut sets

## Change the active shortcut set

1. Make sure there are no other papers open if you want the trick to work for all of them.
2. Click Edit and then Keyboard Shortcuts.
3. From the Set menu, choose a button set. To give you an example, choose Shortcuts for QuarkXPress® 4.0.
4. Click the OK button.

## View shortcuts

1. Click Edit and then Keyboard Shortcuts.
2. Pick a quick set for Set.
3. Choose the place with the directions you want to see in the Product place.
4. Pick an order from the list of commands. In the Current link area, the link is shown.

## Generate a list of shortcuts for printing

1. Click Edit and then Keyboard Shortcuts.
2. Pick a quick set for Set.
3. Click on Show Set.

**All of the present and unclear options for that set are shown in a text file when it starts.**

## Create a new shortcut set

1. Click Edit and then Keyboard Shortcuts.
2. Press "New Set."
3. Give the new set a name and choose an alternative set from the Based On Set menu. Then click OK to finish.

## Create or redefine a shortcut

1. Click Edit and then Keyboard Shortcuts.
2. Click on Set and pick a shortcut set, or click on New Set to make a new one.

**Note:** You can't change the button sets for Default or QuarkXPress. Make a new set based on one of these sets instead, and then change the new set.

3. In the Product Area, choose the area that has the order you want to create or change.
4. Choose the command you want to create or change from the list of commands.
5. In the box that says "New Shortcut," press the keys that you want to use again and again. InDesign shows the other command under Current Shortcuts if the key sequence is already being used for another command. You could also change the first option, or you could try a different one.

**Note:** You shouldn't give menu options single-key shortcuts because they get in the way of typing text. If there is an entry point visible when you type a single-key shortcut, InDesign will use the shortcut instead of adding the character to the text.

6. In the list of contexts, choose the one where you want the computer action to work. The context makes sure that the tool does what you want it to do. You can use Ctrl+G to join table cells (Table context) and Ctrl+G to add special characters (Text context), for example.

**Note:** You should assign tools in the Default context if you want them to work no matter what the document is doing at the moment. When you set shortcuts in a different context, like Table or

Text, they take precedence over the shortcuts set in the Default context.

7. **Pick one of these options:**
   - Click "Assign" to make a new path where there isn't one already.
   - If you want to add another option to an action, click "Assign." There may be more than one computer option for a menu action.
8. Click OK to close the box, or click Save to keep it open while you add more links.

# Hidden Features and Productivity Hacks

1. **Create a Style Sheet for your styles**

The most useful thing about InDesign is its paragraph style. Adding this option can make you much more productive and cut down on the time you spend organizing your files. Even though many people who use InDesign know how useful paragraph styles are and how they can help them make better layouts and save a lot of time, they still don't use them. Why does that happen? It can be hard to keep track of all the styles in a document, and sometimes it may not seem to make much sense. But styles are very important if you want to keep your look uniform, make changes that work well, or use tools like Hyperlinks or Table of Contents. Over the years, I designed my styles in a way that worked well for me, and I noticed that I used the same format in all of my papers. Even though I used the same approach every time, it took me about 3 to 4 hours to organize my styles for a typical job. That wasn't worth the time because I kept making the same layout over and over again. The font families used for the titles and the body were the little things that were always changing. Other small things that changed were things like spaces before paragraphs and so on.

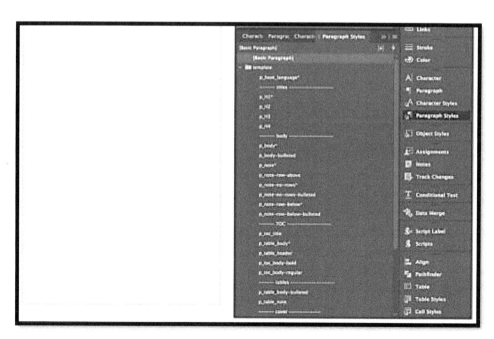

You can start a project right from the Style Sheet, or you can use it as a guide to make an InDesign file and then import the styles from that file. This first InDesign tip cut my start-up time from three to four hours to an hour or even less. You'll also make sure that all of your styles are set up correctly and that no setting is missing (for example, language, hyphenation), and by setting up "based on" and "next style" in your paragraph styles, you'll be able to speed up the whole process of making the document.

2. **Use InDesign templates**

People who work on a lot of papers with the same style or even content, like a user guide, a magazine, a newspaper, etc., might want to turn the Style Sheet idea we saw above into templates and add master pages, borders, grid lines, common parts, and so on. An InDesign template is a file that opens as a new, blank page when it is opened.

One clear benefit of starting a project from a template is that it saves time. It's also great when working with others because it makes sure that everyone starts from the same place. When working as a team, having files with the same structure also helps everyone work faster on the document. Naturally, you don't have to just work on your papers. You can also get an InDesign design (the link has the best one I could find online) and start working from that.

# Quickly lay out the information

Once you have a solid base for your project, the next step is to quickly add the information to your paper. Even though paragraph styles are very important, there are other tools that can assist you whether you are writing in InDesign for a book, a user guide, a catalog, or just for fun.

### 3. Use the primary text option

The text usually comes from a Word or RTF file that has already been organized. This is especially true for books and user guides. Then it's up to you to add this text to your paper and style it correctly. You know how long it takes to make all the pages and make sure the text flows right in the paper if you've done it before. This is something that InDesign can do for you. You can import the text with just a few clicks, and InDesign will make the pages and linked text frames for you. Just like magic!

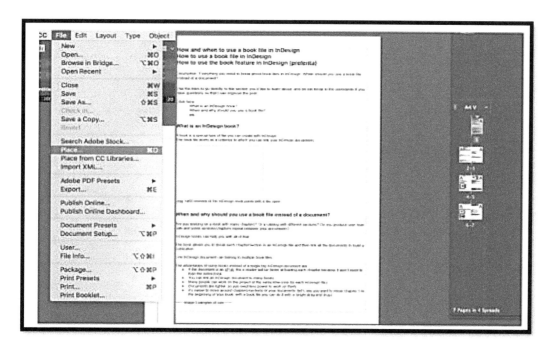

To do this, you need to set up your master pages, add a text frame to each master page, thread the text, and turn on the "**Primary Text Frame**" function. After that, you can bring the text into InDesign. This process can save you a lot of time and make the process of loading your text almost entirely automatic.

### 4. Data merge

Data join is a great way to save time, but a lot of people who use InDesign don't know about it. From a worksheet and a template, data merge lets you quickly arrange hundreds of pages with a "**repetitive layout**." These pages could be business cards, awards, or even catalogs. It speeds up the process, makes sure the plan is uniform, keeps me from making mistakes, and lets me give some jobs to my client. I use it every time I make a catalog.

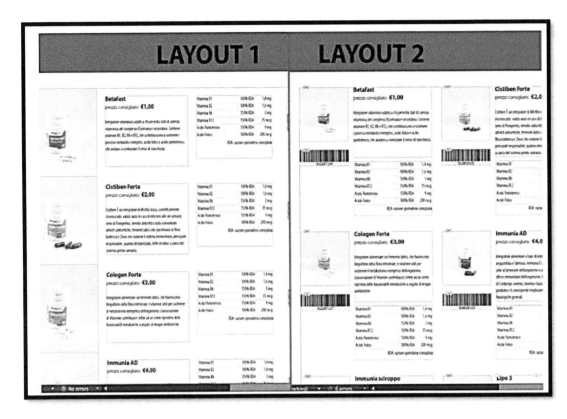

When you make a list again, think about how it will be laid out and where you will put each piece of information. Split the file into several parts if you need more examples. Please have your client or coworker fill out an Excel file with the information you need. Then, make sure the file is ready to be used in the data merge process.

### 5. Use "Next Style"

We've seen how to add text or data to an InDesign project. But what if you pasted some text and want to quickly set the styles? This is another time when Paragraph Styles save the day and make things go more quickly and easily. We've seen that adding paragraph styles to your text can make it look great and uniform. You can give many chosen lines different styles with the **"Next Style"** feature. When you type in InDesign, "Next Style" also works. "Return" will tell InDesign to use the "Next Style" you chose for the new paragraph.

### 6. Learn how to use Anchored Object

When you anchor items in InDesign, you can make amazing automation. For instance, you could make a sign whose width changes immediately when the text does.

### 7. Use book files

It's also true that very few people use eBook files. If you want to keep all of your InDesign files together, you can use a book as a collection.

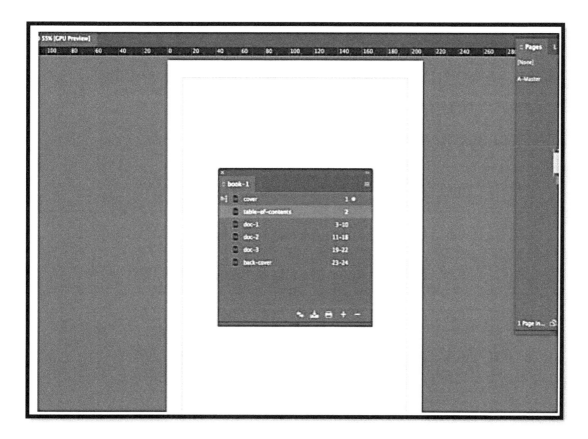

Book files let you divide a publication into smaller pieces that are easier to work on. This also lets other people at work work on the same document, since it's split up into different files.

8. **Use PDF presets**

A PDF setup is a set of options that change how a PDF is made. Some settings in InDesign work for some designers, but not all of them make sense. It might be helpful to make your setup if you need to change the PDF export setting a lot, like when you want to add Marks or Bleeds. You can easily make your setting from the PDF export box. Make changes to the settings, then click "Save Preset." This simple tip might not save hours the first time you use it, but it will save you time every time. You will also make sure you don't forget to change any settings.

# CHAPTER 14
# COMMON ISSUES AND SOLUTIONS

## Troubleshooting Document Errors

### Color Management Challenges

**Identifying Issues:**
1. There are color differences throughout the whole paper (Paper 1).
2. Spot colors or changing between RGB and CMYK color modes don't work right.

**How to Fix:**
1. Use the "Preflight" screen to find and fix color problems, making sure that the document has a pleasant and consistent color scheme.
2. Make sure that all of the document's parts use the same color profiles. Differences in color profiles could confuse or distract readers.
3. If the paper is going to be printed, change the RGB pictures to CMYK. This step makes sure that the file will work with the printing process and that the colors will stay true.

### Text Overflow Challenges

**Identifying Issues:**
1. The text goes beyond the edges of the text box that was set up.

**How to Fix:**
1. To quickly find cases of overflow, use the "Overset Text" sign in the bottom-right area of text frames.
2. Change the size of text frames or the text inside them to make sure it fits correctly in the frame.

## Image Quality Concerns

**Identifying Issues:**
1. Some of the links in the "Links" part are missing or broken, which could make the page harder to view and use.
2. The pixelation in some pictures is caused by low quality, which makes the pictures look bad and less clear overall.

**How to Fix:**
1. Make sure the "Links" area works by checking for and fixing any broken or missing links to make the user experience smooth.
2. Use the "Links" area to check the quality of a picture and make it better. To keep your presentation looking professional and nice to look at, replace pictures with smaller quality.
3. Think about how adding pictures or giving a high-resolution version when saving to PDF will affect people who are viewing from outside the document. This technique makes the

paper look better and easier to read generally.

**Additional Considerations:**
- Check and update links often to keep information up-to-date and trustworthy.
- Use software for changing pictures to make the quality better, which will make them look more finished and professional.
- Work with the people who are making the material to make sure that the pictures meet high standards. This will help make the show look good and flow well.

## Layering Challenges

**Identifying Issues**:
1. The visible ordering is broken because the layers are in the wrong order.

**How to Fix:**
1. Look over the layers panel to find and fix any problems with the order of the levels so that the visual structure is smooth.
2. Put layers in the right order to improve the design's general structure and flow.
3. Use the "Layers" tab to control which items can be seen, and make sure that parts are on the right levels and in the right order.

**Additional Considerations:**
- Check the layer structure often to make sure it can adapt to changes and improvements in the design.
- Use the layers panel's grouping and naming rules to make your work and teamwork go more smoothly.
- Work with your team to make sure that everyone is using the same layering style, especially on projects with a lot of workers.

# Recovering from crashes and unexpected issues

It can be annoying when Adobe InDesign crashes or acts up for no reason, but there are things you can do to get your work back and figure out what's wrong. **Here is a guide to help you get back to normal after Adobe InDesign crashes or does something strange:**

1. **Turn on Auto-Recovery:**
   - In Windows, go to Edit > Preferences > File Handling; in Mac, go to InDesign > Preferences > File Handling.
   - Check the box next to "Automatically Save Recovery Data Every" and choose how often to save the data. This makes sure that InDesign backs up itself automatically.
2. **Check the Auto-Recovery Folder:** If InDesign crashes, it may have saved a recovery file. Find a file with the name ".indd" in the Auto-Recovery folder (the Preferences tell you where to find it).
3. **Save Incrementally:** Save your work regularly using incremental file names, like Project_v1.indd and Project_v2.indd. This makes several copies of the file in case it crashes, and you can go back to the most recent copy.
4. **Use file recovery services:** Adobe InDesign has a tool that lets you get back papers that

you haven't saved yet. Click File, then Open Recent, and then click Recover Unsaved Documents. This could help you get back to recent changes.

5. **Turn off third-party plugins:** Crashes can be caused by third-party plugins that don't work with the main program or are broken. Turn off plugins for now to see if the problem still exists. In Windows, go to Edit > Preferences > Plugins. On a Mac, go to InDesign > Preferences > Plugins.

6. **Update InDesign:** Make sure you have the most recent version of Adobe InDesign. Updates often fix bugs and make improvements that can fix problems with stability.

7. **Check System Requirements:** Make sure your computer meets the system requirements for the version of InDesign you are using. The system requirements can be found here. Crashes can happen when the system doesn't have enough resources.

8. **Clear InDesign Cache:** Cache files that are damaged can cause problems you didn't expect. To clear the InDesign cache, start InDesign and hold down Ctrl + Alt + Shift (Windows) or Cmd + Opt + Shift (Mac).

9. **Create a New Document:** Open a brand-new, empty document and try pasting parts of the crashed document into it. This can help you narrow down the problem to a certain page or feature.

10. **Contact Adobe Support:** If the situation keeps happening, get in touch with Adobe Support. They can help you and may know about problems and answers that only happen with your version of InDesign.

# Optimizing InDesign performance for large documents

We wish things would always go as smoothly and quickly as we'd like, but they don't always. Following some testing steps and being sure that the issue is not with a specific file or an object inside that file, there are a few things you can try to make InDesign run faster. And you know that your computer can usually handle the heavy work you have going on, then one or three of these issues and settings in InDesign could be stopping your machine from working right.

## Set InDesign's Display Performance to Typical

The amount of processing power used goes up when you look at pictures at a high quality because InDesign has to keep redrawing parts as you move around the page. If you go to InDesign/Edit > Preferences > Display Performance and set the preset to Typical, the pictures will be shown at a quality that is good for screens. For a very long time, this has been the usual way for InDesign to show pictures on the screen. On the other hand, it looks like the most current version always sets to High Quality. It is possible to change how the present text is displayed if you right-click or control-click on a page. Another way to change the setting for just one picture is to right-click or control-click on it. This is still possible even when the sensitivity is set to high by default.

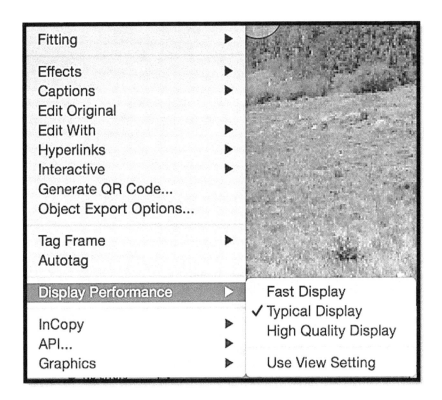

## Turn off Live Drawing

If you want to get things done faster, turn off Live Screen Drawing in InDesign or at least set it to Delayed in the Interface tab of your Preferences. If you choose the "delayed" choice, you can see what the change will look like as you do it. If you click on an object, like a picture, and then wait a very short time before moving or changing it, this will happen. If you choose this choice right away, InDesign will have to show you each step of the process for each change. There is a lot of work to do.

## Minimize Live Preflight

When you set the preferences for a certain result, Live Preflight works in the background to make sure that your document meets those preferences. It's probably working if you're not working. You can limit the pages that the Preflight panel looks at when you open it. The menu bar lets you do this by selecting **Window > Output > Preflight**. Alternatively, you can hit the Preflight option to the right of the red or green dot at the bottom of the document frame. Click on the radio button to the right of the "All" option at the bottom of the screen to choose a page or a different style. As of right now, the pre-flighting is only happening on that one page. Even better, you can turn it off totally by deselecting the "On" choice until the time you are ready to preflight.

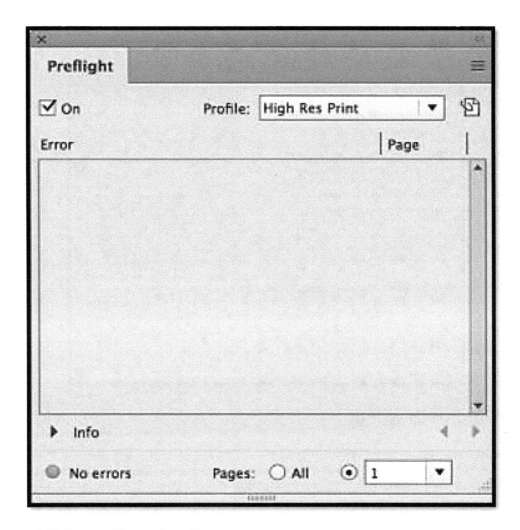

## Turn Off Page Thumbnails

The pictures in your Pages box are working hard to keep up with you if your document has a lot of pages and each page has a lot of things on it. Even if they are redrawing, the images are not very useful because the page icons are often so small. For the most part, this is the case. To stop thumbnails from showing up on both pages and masters, go to the Pages panel menu and select Panel Options. Then, uncheck the box next to Show Thumbnails.

## Turn Off Hyperlink Verification

There is a chance that a file with a lot of hyperlinks will load much more slowly because InDesign checks the URLs inside hyperlinks for validity all the time. If you want to stop checking the same URLs over and over, remove the "**Auto Update URL Status**" option from the Hyperlinks panel menu.

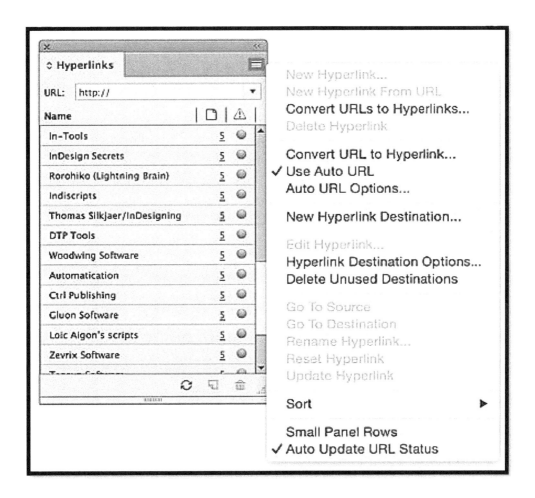

## Disable the Save Preview Images feature

As you save your papers, InDesign gives you the choice to include a sample picture, which is also what it does by default. This is another thing that is always being changed while you are working. To make changes to this item, go to the Preferences menu and select the File Handling pane. By unchecking the "Always Save Preview Images" box, you can turn off the feature. At the very least, you could limit the sample pages to only the first one or two pages of the text. You could also limit the size of the preview itself.

# CHAPTER 15
# ADVANCED TYPOGRAPHY TECHNIQUES

## OpenType Features

- First, pick a font that works with OpenType features. A lot of modern and professional fonts offer a lot of stylistic choices.
- The names of OpenType fonts often tell you what they can do, like *"Pro," "Std,"* or *"OpenType."*

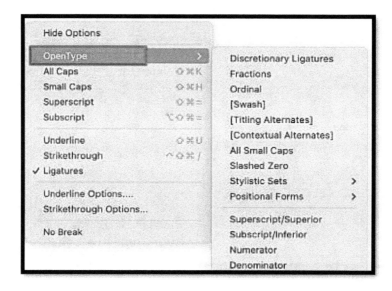

- You can get to the Glyphs panel in InDesign by going to **Window > Type & Tables > Glyphs**.
- This panel lets you see and type in single glyphs, including those with special characters and ligatures.
- Ligatures are groups of two or more characters that are meant to look better when they are used together. In the Character box, select the word and choose the "Ligatures" choice. This will make the ligatures appear.
- There are swashes and other symbols in some fonts that can be found in the Glyphs panel. Look for people who have beautiful flair.
- The Stylistic Sets choice in the Character panel lets you pick from some different sets of styling options for characters.
- "Contextual alternatives" are character types that are changed instantly based on the other characters around them. In the OpenType panel, contextual options can be turned on or off.
- A lot of the time, OpenType fonts have special characters for working with fractions. The Glyphs panel or the Fraction choice in the Character panel can be used to get to these.
- True small caps, which are meant to look and feel like capital letters, can be used with

OpenType. From the Character menu, choose the text you want to change and click on the "tiny Caps" button.

- To get to special characters like ordinals (1st, 2nd, and 3rd) or superscripts and subscripts, use the Glyphs or Character windows.
- You might want to add OpenType features to the Paragraph and Character Styles so that they are used the same way every time. This makes sure that the styles are applied the same way everywhere on your page.
- If you want to see how your document will look with OpenType features added, use InDesign's Preview mode. When you export your file, like PDF, make sure you choose the "embed fonts" option so that the OpenType features stay in the final file.

# Implementing ligatures, swashes, and alternate characters

A normal ligature in fonts takes two or three characters and puts them together to make one. This kind of ligature helps with kerning when one character moves into the space left by the next character. In each tongue, there are different ligatures. This is because many words in English use the letters ff, ffi, fi, and fl together. When you use ligatures, be careful because they can stand out a lot if your text has a lot of space between the letters.

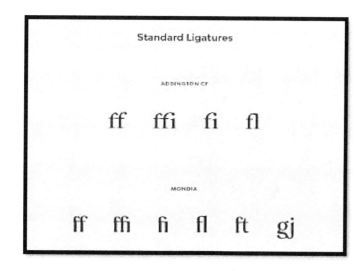

Another kind of ligature is an optional ligature, which is usually just for looks. Also, these ligatures join two or three characters together to make a single, beautiful design. There are combinations like TH, th, ck, ct, et, and st. There are also double characters like oo, tt, and ll. This kind of binding needs to be used carefully, just like any other kind. It's important to make it clear that not all fonts have standard and optional ligatures. Each font is unique, and it's up to the font creator to decide which ones to use.

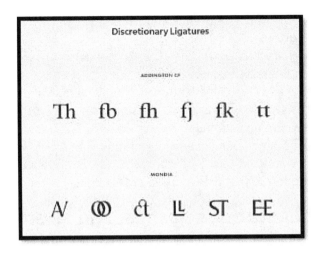

# How to Use Ligatures in InDesign

### Step 1

Make a new file in Adobe InDesign by opening it. To get to the Glyphs panel, go to Window > Type > Glyphs. To turn ligatures on or off, go to **Window > Type > Character** and open the Character box. To turn them on or off, click the button in the upper right spot and choose Ligatures.

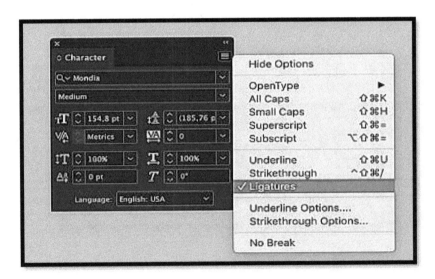

### Step 2

Pick up the Text Tool (T) from the menu bar and type anything you want. I'll use "THE TWIN MOON INN" for this lesson. Change the font to Mondia.

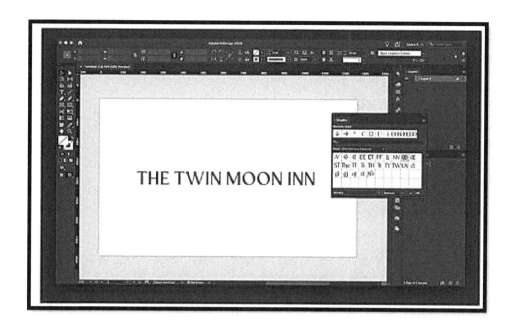

**Step 3**

Set the group of icons to Standard Ligatures in the icons panel. Use the **Text Tool (T)** to choose the pair of characters you want to change in the Glyphs box. Then, use the ligatures. In the Glyphs panel, double-click on the style you want to use. If you want the ligatures to show up immediately, make sure you turn them on in the Character box.

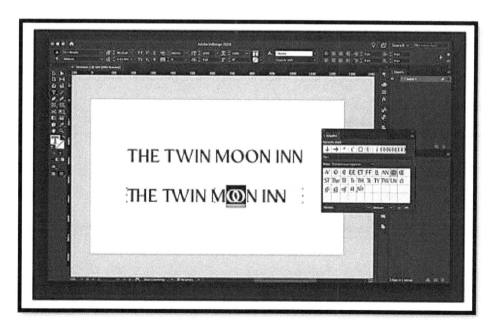

# Access Alternate Characters in InDesign?

## Option #1 – Select a letter

**For different people, this works.**

1. Pick out the letter you want to change.
2. If there is a different image, a small box will appear.
3. Click on the different option you want to add.

## Option #2 – Access via the glyphs panel

**For different letters and ligatures, this works.**

1. Go to the top menu and choose **Type > Glyphs or Window > Type & Tables > Glyphs**.
2. In the upper right corner, choose the type you want to use.
3. Select a letter or use the type tool to select a character, and then click on a character you want to add.

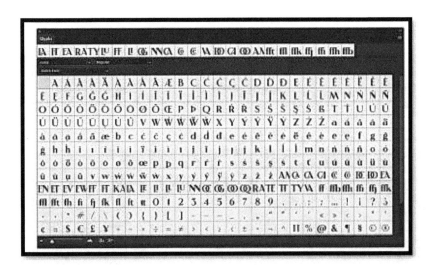

# Establishing an effective typographic hierarchy

Setting up a good typography order in Adobe InDesign is important for making papers that look good and are easy to read. Typographic order organizes and ranks information to help the reader find their way through the text. **To set up a strong stylistic order in Adobe InDesign, follow these tips:**

1. **Heading Styles:**
   - Put different amounts of information under different heading styles (e.g., Heading 1, Heading 2, etc.).
   - Use the same font family, size, and color for all levels of headings.

- Change the leading (line spacing) to make it easy to tell the difference between headers and body text.
2. **Font Choice:**
   - Use a few different fonts to keep the look professional and unified.
   - Pick styles that go well with each other. It is normal to use a serif font with a sans-serif script.
3. **Font Size:**
   - Use bigger font sizes for more important information and smaller ones for less important information.
   - Lower-level titles and body text should have font sizes that are gradually smaller.
4. **Font Weight:**
   - Use different font weights (like normal, bold, and light) to draw attention to and away from writing.
   - Make sure that the difference in weight is clear but not too much.
5. **Color:**
   - Smartly use color to draw attention to certain parts. As an example, you could use a bright color for the headings and a dull color for the text.
   - Make sure the difference in color between the text and the background is big enough to read.
6. **Spacing:**
   - Change the distance between lines (leading) and between letters (tracking) to make the text easier to read.
   - Make good use of white space (like borders and gaps) to make the plan look clean and well-organized.
7. **Alignment:** Align the text in the same way all over the page. Based on how the text looks, you can choose between left, center, right, or justified orientation.
8. **Consistency:**
   - Use the same fonts and styles throughout the whole paper to make it look professional and put together.
   - Set a flow by using the same font types and sizes for parts that go together.
9. **Hierarchy with Scale:** Use a scale of letter sizes to make a clear visual order. For instance, the main titles might be a lot bigger than the subheadings, and so on.
10. **Contrast:**
    - To draw attention to important information, use contrast by changing the font size, weight, and style.
    - Play around with different combos until you find one that looks good and works well.
11. **Preview and Adjust:**
    - Look over your paper often to make sure the font structure is clear and uniform.
    - Make changes as needed based on what people say and what you can see.

# CHAPTER 16
# CUSTOMIZING INDESIGN WITH SCRIPTS AND EXTENSIONS

## Create, install, and manage plugins

The InDesign plugin modules are pieces of software made by Adobe and other companies that work with Adobe to add extra features. There are a lot of importing, exporting, scripting, and special effects plugins that come with your program and are set up immediately in the Plugins area. Plugins are what give you most of the tools you see in InDesign.

### Install plugins

**Plugin modules show up as choices on menus, dialogs, or windows after they are enabled.**

1. Use the launcher that comes with the plugin module if one is given. If not, take a copy of the module and drag it into the Plugins folder inside the InDesign application folder.
2. Follow any directions that come with the app for setting it up.

**Note:** You can use any paid tool that is made to work with InDesign. Adobe Technical Support can help you figure out which apps are causing the problem. If, on the other hand, it turns out that the problem is caused by a plug-in made by a different company, you'll need to get help from that company.

### Create InDesign plugins with UXP

It is now possible to use current JavaScript (ES5 and most of ES6) in InDesign plugins thanks to the Unified Extensibility Platform (UXP).

## Integration with Creative Cloud Add-ons via the Browse Add-ons menu

**Within the Adobe Exchange website, you can look for and set up add-ons, apps, and more for Adobe InDesign and other programs.**

- To add the extra tools to InDesign, go to **Window > Browse Add-ons**. You can get these extras for free or for a fee. This process syncs all the tools you've downloaded or updated from the Creative Cloud app for InDesign with InDesign. It gets you to the page where you can view add-ons.
- You can then see these add-ons in Window > Extensions, Downloads, or the place stated in the add-on's description. Go to the explore add-ons page and look for "View my add-

ons" in the menu on the left. This will show you the add-ons you've downloaded. It also shows which items and versions of those goods these add-ons work with.

If you turn on file sync, the search add-ons will connect to your Creative Cloud account.

## Installing and Managing Extensions

You can add different features to InDesign by installing plugins. To do this, you must first go to Adobe's website. In this case, you need to use exchange.adobe.com. If you look for this Adobe page, it will show up. Go to the "Creative Cloud" tab on this page. On this page, scroll down and pick InDesign from the list of goods. It will show you all the tools that work with InDesign once you choose it. You could also open InDesign and go to the Windows menu. Choose "Find Extensions on Exchange" from the list that comes up.

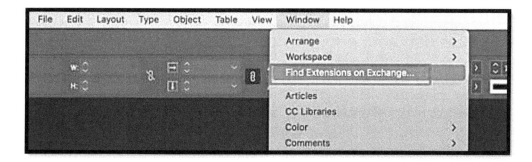

If you pick that choice, InDesign will take you to the website for the Adobe InDesign app. It will ask you to log in if you are not already. Then, click the "Free" button to make it possible to install. It will ask you to agree to the terms and conditions, which you should do. There will also be a box that says "Install." Click that. If you have any issues, please visit the Installation help part of this page. You will be taken to this page when you choose the "help" choice. From this page, you can download the given application right away. If you click on Download, you will get an installation file. Then, follow the steps below to properly install the app you chose. Install the raw file with Adobe's Creative Cloud PC program once you have it in the format you want. Now it will take you to the page where you can download the extension manager. Here is where you can click to download.

After you've gotten it, put it in. When you put it in, it will look like this. In this window box, the Install tab is in the top left area. Click on it. When you click the Install button, a new box will show up where you can pick the installation file for the extension you chose. When the extension manager is done running, it will show a message that says "successfully installed." If the application you installed is not where you thought it would be in InDesign, go back to the page where you installed it. You'll see the words "Where to discover It'll" further down. You can read the writing by clicking on it, and this is where you can find this extension in your InDesign program. If you already have InDesign open, close it and then open it again to see the changes. Then, go to the Window menu. In its drop-down menu, we can choose "Extension." Your added app will show up in the sub-drop-down menu.

## Removing an InDesign Extension

We no longer need a few of the tools they came with, so we need to remove them from our program for different reasons. Here's what you can do to make it happen. If you used the InDesign Creative Cloud app to add your extension, use the extension manager to open it. When you open one of them, a list of everything you've loaded will show up. Pick out what you want to get rid of. Once you've picked the one you want, click the "Remove" button in this box. It will only take a few seconds to remove the app you picked. The old extension might still be in the list of loaded extensions if you check it again in InDesign. This is because you have to restart the app to see the changes.

# Frequently Asked Questions

## What is InDesign and who is it for?

Adobe InDesign is a complex program for workers who work with both paper and digital printing to lay out pages. The software comes with all the tools you need to create, test, and share a wide range of material for print, the web, and tablet apps, among other formats. Users of InDesign can fine-tune fonts, use creative tools that come with the program, and work in an easy-to-use design environment. The software works well with other Adobe products, like Photoshop, Illustrator, Acrobat, and Adobe Animate, making it easy for creative workers to get their work done. A wide range of people can use InDesign, such as artists, people who work in prepress and production, and print service providers. People who work in magazines, design firms, advertising agencies, newspapers, book publishers, retail/catalog companies, business design, commercial printing, and other advanced publishing settings are among its target audience. The app meets the specific needs of these workers by giving them a strong base for making papers that look good and are well organized. One big benefit of using InDesign is that it is part of the Adobe Creative Cloud environment. As soon as new changes and releases are ready, subscribers can get them. This makes sure that users always have access to the newest features and improvements. Users with a Creative Cloud All Apps plan can also use Adobe Digital Publishing Suite, Single Edition* with InDesign. This lets them create and package an endless number of single-edition iPad apps that can be uploaded to the Apple App Store.

## How does InDesign integrate with other Adobe products?

It's not just a technology merger; Photoshop, Illustrator, Flash Professional, and InDesign all use the same user interface, instructions, panels, and tools. The shared framework makes learning easier for users because they can use what they know from one program when switching to another. Moving quickly between Adobe programs is easy thanks to the uniform design, which makes the experience smooth and natural. One of the best things about InDesign's inclusion is that you can easily load Photoshop and Illustrator files. Using this feature makes it easier to lay out, improve, and update images in the InDesign setting. Users can easily add files from these programs, which keep the design's purity and reduces the amount of work needed to handle visual elements. Another useful aspect of InDesign is that it can directly open PDF files. This makes sure that the output is reliable and uniform across all printing forms, such as print, web, and smartphones. This support makes it easier to share and keeps the look of papers the same no matter what output source is picked. InDesign and Flash Professional work well together, so users can easily move page layouts between the two programs while keeping any motion, sound, or video files that are contained in the documents. This makes sure that the quality stays good when switching between the two programs, giving you a smooth multimedia experience. Also, InDesign and InCopy work together to give small creative teams a powerful editing process management system. This teamwork makes it easier for artists and writers to work together and talk to each other. It also speeds up the editing process and makes content creation more efficient and team-based.

## What is the InDesign family of products?

The main product of a combined publishing family is Adobe InDesign. It is joined by InCopy and InDesign Server. This connected environment is made to help with different parts of the publishing process by giving you specific tools for writing, rewriting, working together, and using server-based solutions. InCopy is a professional writing and editing tool that works well with InDesign and is an important part of this family. The main goal is to make it easier for artists, writers, and editors to work together on editing processes. By working together with InDesign, InCopy makes it easy for everyone involved in the content creation process to work together. The artistic Cloud All Apps plan gives users full access to Adobe's full suite of artistic tools, and InCopy is one of them. InDesign Server is the most advanced member of the family; it adds writing and layout features to a server platform. This new feature adds a higher level of automation to editing processes, making material, customizable printing based on data, and web-to-print solutions that use templates. InDesign Server is made to make things bigger and easier. It has advanced workflow features that make huge printing settings more efficient and productive. When used together, InDesign, InCopy, and InDesign Server make a strong environment that meets the many needs of printing pros. This unified method lets work move smoothly from writing and editing content to advanced composition and automatic publication, making the publishing process faster and easier for everyone to work on together. This Adobe publishing family has a lot of tools and solutions to meet the needs of current content creation and release, whether you are working on a single project or a large-scale publication.

## Does InDesign provide a solution for large publishing environments?

Yes. Systems developers around the world can offer printing systems that work with both InDesign and InCopy if you need a custom solution built on core InDesign technology.

## Should QuarkXPress users convert to InDesign?

Yes. InDesign has been used by publishers all over the world, from small design groups to large printing companies. InDesign is the best choice for printing settings that move quickly because it has a strong partner community, is backed by an industry leader, and is user-driven.

## In what languages can InDesign files be created and shared?

You can open and change Indic, Japanese, Middle Eastern, Chinese, and Korean layouts in Roman and Indic versions of InDesign. You can also do the same with Japanese, Middle Eastern, Chinese, or Korean versions of Roman and Indic files. But the Roman versions of InDesign don't have the stylistic, layout grid, and frame grid tools that the Japanese, Middle Eastern, Chinese, and Korean versions do. These tools are needed to change text in the Middle East and Asia.

## What is an InDesign Server?

With InDesign Server, you can manage the design, layout, and typography features of InDesign. It is a strong, highly flexible, and scalable layout and composition engine. It uses the same code base as InDesign and can run a lot of different automatic printing solutions, such as web-to-print, VDP, and editing workflow solutions. It also gives you the same high-quality output as InDesign. Most systems that use InDesign Server are based on models that designers made with the desktop version of InDesign.

## How does InDesign differ from InDesign Server?

**There are some important changes between InDesign Server and the PC version of InDesign, even though they share the same code base:**

- InDesign Server is a tool that runs bigger automatic printing systems.
- InDesign Server is an empty program, which means it doesn't have a user interface built in. A customer or a solution partner would make a user interface that works with the automatic printing system that InDesign Server runs.
- You can use scripts or C++ plug-ins to control InDesign Server, just like you can with InDesign. It can be controlled by a SOAP interface or Java APIs, though. You can also use the Flex framework and Adobe Flash Builder (sold separately) to create interesting rich Internet applications (RIAs) that run in web browsers or as stand-alone clients with the Adobe AIR runtime. The scalable and reliable back-end server is the InDesign Server.
- Automated printing systems that use InDesign Server can grow as needed because they can run multiple versions on different computers.
- InDesign Server has been tried thoroughly to help make sure it works well for long amounts of time.
- InDesign Server was made to work on server versions of Windows and Mac OS, including Microsoft Windows Server 2008 R2.
- You can't get an InDesign Server with Creative Cloud; you have to buy it separately.

# Conclusion

Finally, this Adobe InDesign guide has given you the tools you need to be creative and make designs that look great. You now have the skills you need to confidently use InDesign, from knowing how to use the software's interface to exploring its more advanced features. You can use the guidelines in this guide as a guide whether you're making interesting print materials or digital content. Always keep in mind that InDesign is more than just a tool; it's a blank slate for your creativity. Accept the creative process, try out different methods, and let your imagination grow. With the information in this help, you should be able to turn ideas into plans that look good. As you start to work with design, use Adobe InDesign to make your ideas come to life, and enjoy the process of making content that is interesting and has an effect. Good luck with your Designs!

# INDEX

**D**

## S

---

# T

## U

www.ingramcontent.com/pod-product-compliance
Lightning Source LLC
La Vergne TN
LVHW081525050326
832903LV00025B/1636